The Insurance Field Book of Commercial Insurance

by Fouad Husseini

Published by Fouad Husseini

Copyright © 2017 by Fouad Husseini, BEng., ACII

All rights reserved. No part of this publication may be reproduced, distributed, or transmitted in any form or by any means, including photocopying, recording, or other electronic or mechanical methods, without the prior written permission of the publisher, except in the case of brief quotations embodied in critical reviews and certain other noncommercial uses permitted by copyright law. For permission requests, please write to the publisher.

Ordering Information Quantity sales. Special discounts are available on quantity purchases by corporations, associations, and others. For details, contact the publisher at https://insurancefieldbook.com

Printed and assembled in the United States of America

First printing: 2017

The Insurance Field Book™. All rights reserved.

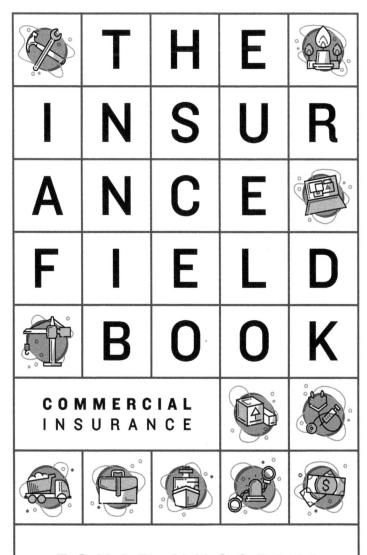

Contents

Preface XI

SECTION 1: Fundamental Elements of Insurance

01. Introduction 3

02. The Brief History of Insurance 7

03. Understanding the Anatomy of The
    Insurance Policy 11

04. Insurance Underwriting Practices and Concepts 15

05. Policy Deductibles 19

06. Replacement Value (Cost Value) v
    Actual Cash Value (Market Value) 23

07. Under-insurance and The Application
    of Average 27

08. "Claims Made" and "Claims Occurring" Policies 31

09. Supplementing Insurance Coverage ... 35

SECION 2: Insurance Policy Coverage Explained

10. The Commercial Auto Insurance Policy ... 41

11. The Burglary Insurance Policy ... 51

12. The Business Interruption Insurance Policy ... 57

13. The Marine Cargo insurance Policy ... 67

14. The Carrier's Liability Insurance Policy ... 77

15. The Commercial General Liability Insurance Policy ... 85

16. The Contractors/Erection All Risks Insurance Policies ... 93

17. The Contractors Plant and Equipment Insurance Policy ... 103

18. The Cyber Liability Insurance Policy ... 111

19. The Deterioration of Stock insurance Policy ... 121

20. Directors and Officers Liability Insurance Policy ... 129

21. The Electronic Equipment Insurance Policy ... 137

22. The Employers Liability Insurance Policy ... 145

23. The Environmental Liability Insurance Policy ... 153

24. The Fidelity Guarantee Insurance Policy ... 163

25. The Fire Insurance Policy ... 171

26. The Group Life Insurance Policy 179

27. The Marine Hull and Machinery Insurance Policy 187

28. The Inland Transit Insurance Policy 195

29. The Key Person Insurance Policy 203

30. The Equipment Breakdown Insurance Policy 211

31. The Medical Malpractice Insurance Policy 219

32. The Money Insurance Policy 227

33. The Group Personal Accident Insurance Policy 235

34. The Property All Risks Insurance Policy 243

35. The Professional Indemnity Insurance Policy 251

36. The Products Liability Insurance Policy 259

37. The Property Terrorism and Sabotage Insurance Policy 269

38. The Trade Credit Insurance policy 279

39. The Workmen Compensation Insurance Policy 289

SECTION 3: The Wider Picture

40. Know Your Customer (KYC) 301

41. Code of Ethics 305

42. Insurance Intermediaries 309

43. Professional Qualifications … 319

44. Risk Management … 323

45. Reinsurance … 327

SECTION 4: Four Ways Insurance is Getting Ahead in a Digital World

Blockchain … 337

Just-in-Time insurance … 339

Wearable Devices … 340

Peer-to-Peer (P2P) insurance … 342

Bibliography … 345

THE INSURANCE
FIELD BOOK

Preface

This book started as an idea to create an instructor-less manual for insurance agents and brokers starting out in the commercial insurance field. I was always asked for book recommendations and additional readings and my answers usually indicated either too much technical reading or missed the mark.

Unfortunately there was no single book that satisfied their needs. Those that ventured into reading available material returned with questions and conflicting advice. Some were more confused than when they started.

This led me to think of how I could consolidate my experience with the aid of research and real life examples to satisfy the needs of the learner and to also add something new to this field. I sought to provide a pragmatic approach without trying to reinvent the wheel.

The Insurance Field Book raises awareness of the different processes and choices available in selling or purchasing insurance coverage. I reluctantly had to exclude complex or rather technical aspects of insurance which was difficult at times given my technical background but pragmatic consistency meant that the book should not be intimidating nor a mammoth reading challenge.

The material has been thoroughly researched and includes latest research findings available at the time of writing. I would emphasize that the period from 2015 to 2017 is well represented in this book providing a wealth of up to date surveys and research findings.

Readers gaining this foundational level of knowledge will be able make more informed choices about the different insurance coverages. A total of 30 different commercial policies are dissected for your pleasure! Each policy description is intended to provide an outline of the scheme and an overview of some of the limitations that apply.

Finally, I don't believe anyone is able to produce a body of work without building on the knowledge that others have labored to conceive. I would like to thank the many individuals and companies that have provided their permission for me to use their work in my book, most notably, Allianz Global Corporate & Specialty, Prudential Financial Inc., The British Medical Journal (BMJ), Intrum Justitia, Allen & Overy, and others.

Section 1

Fundamental Elements of Insurance

"Information is not knowledge. The only source of knowledge is experience."

Albert Einstein

SECTION I

01

Introduction

For most people insurance products are difficult to understand and evaluate. Some insurance products can seem like a commodity, with the only significant variable being price. But this is not entirely true. While there is considerable standardization in insurance policies, this standardization is far from absolute. It is important to understand what is covered under the policy and what is excluded.

Insurance is a tool to protect a business against a variety of risks and I would argue that it also increases its value. It provides financial recourse to its investors, directors, customers and employees. It is therefore a vital component in the armor of any going concern.

Insurance makes funds available to compensate for losses that are incurred from unpredictable or undesirable events.

For a business owner, navigating the range of insurance options available can be daunting at times. It is theoretically possible to obtain insurance for almost any event or

SECTION I

INTRODUCTION

occurrence if there is an insurer willing to provide cover and a business ready to pay the premium.

Different businesses have different insurance needs, and those needs can change over time. The needs of a self-employed person may differ from those who own and operate small businesses with multiple employees. Similarly, global companies face an increasingly complex risk landscape. As well as having to battle the threat posed by natural disasters and manmade hazards, companies also have to deal with the demands of increasingly less forgiving regulatory and legal environments.

Mistakes are a pain to everyone. But for businesses, mistakes are devastating, they expose companies to huge liabilities and tremendous losses.

Unfortunately, the true value of insurance is often only recognized after an unexpected loss had happened. At other times, insurance can be viewed by boards and business managers as just another overhead expense, where great emphasis is placed on securing the lowest premium. Businesses may fail to appreciate the significance of insurance in supporting the overall strategy of the business and the achievement of its objectives.

The complex exercise of selecting the right policy for a business requires understanding the business operation, industry, size, exposures and so forth, which makes the involvement of specialist advisers very important, as they are likely to know the best products to suit their needs. The result would be a more carefully targeted and strategically aligned approach to insurance design and buying that supports the risk appetite of the business and maximizes the value of the insurance coverage, rather than simply minimizing the cost.

Buyers should have access to enough information to make an informed decision before entering into a contract. It is essential that before a contract is signed, insurance agents and brokers provide true and accurate information regarding the purpose of the insurance policy, the terminology used in the contract, what is and is not covered, the estimated price of the insurance policy, the administrative procedure involved in issuing and maintaining the policy and any other information relating to the insurance contract.

To many people starting out in the insurance, it may appear that underwriters pluck a figure out of the air when they prepare an offer! Whilst it may seem like this on occasion, the reality is very different. Pricing an insurance offer can be a complex series of actuarially driven formulas.

This book will be a good ready reference for salesmen, agents, brokers and their respective clients, giving a general overview of the current covers available and their practical application. Here we will try and explain some of the criteria and what influences pricing.

Please note!

The book is, of necessity, general and international in nature. All values will be denominated in United Sates Dollar.

Insurance by definition, is unique to the Insured and more importantly, the conditions prevailing following an insured incident are ultimately variable.

The Insurance Field Book offers this information as the basis for discussion between insurance buyers and their professional advisors. The terms and conditions of the various policies and schemes described herein will vary from one country (or even state) to another therefore the information in this book should not be used as the sole basis of designing or purchasing insurance programs. This book sets out many of the considerations for examining the coverage of the different insurance policies.

SECTION I

INTRODUCTION

The subjects that will be discussed should heighten the reader's awareness of business insurance and encourage to consider carefully the various insurance programs and options available on the market.

The advice of a professional insurance adviser or an insurance broker with knowledge of various insurance schemes will be extremely valuable.

02

The Brief History of Insurance

The insurance concept in its earliest manifestations, emanated from the need of merchants to survive unexpected financial adversity. The money lenders of Babylon, more than 2000 years B.C., sought to protect the capital they invested in travelling merchants against robbery in transit. Greeks and Romans around 600 A.D. collected contributions through societies and guilds to offer primitive forms of medical, life insurance benefits and burial expenses.

Conventional insurance products

Insurance as we know it today was probably developed in Genoa in the 14th century unbundling loans from insurance and therefore creating separate insurance contracts. It is clear to us today that people throughout history have developed different mutual structures to guarantee mutual protection in wealth and adversity.

SECTION I

THE BRIEF HISTORY OF INSURANCE

Europe and England during the middle ages developed the concept further and the types of insurance coverage that gained prominence were marine, fire and life insurance. Again, mutual societies and mutual associations were the normal entities through which insurance transactions were conducted until 1680 when Edward Lloyd's café became an insurance market for marine insurance allowing ship owners, cargo owners and anyone with a financial interest in the goods or ship to buy insurance. To this day, Lloyd's market continues to play an important role in the world of reinsurance and insurance.

Radical transformation has meant that many mutual-type organizations have demutualized. Nowadays, mutual insurers have a relatively small market share which is dominated by joint-stock companies.

The main motivation behind demutualization is usually the desire to better align the financial interests of owners and management, attract high caliber management, greater access to capital, better financial discipline through public scrutiny and significant opportunities arising in the domestic and global financial services marketplace.

Takaful insurance products

Takaful insurance products refer to insurance that is compliant with Shariah law (Islamic law) and is approved by Muslim scholars. It is a system based on the principles of mutual assistance and voluntary contribution, where risks are shared collectively and voluntarily by a group of participants (the policyholders). Conventional insurance is considered to be incompatible with the Shariah which prohibits excessive uncertainty in dealings and investment in interest bearing assets. The first Takaful insurer was founded in Sudan in 1979.

These products, which are already well established in most of Asia and the Middle East, are increasingly becoming available in Western countries as well.

As of 2010, there were an estimated 1.6 billion Muslims around the world, making Islam the world's second largest religion after Christianity. Although many people may associate Islam with countries in the Middle East and North Africa, nearly 62% of Muslims live in the Asia Pacific region, according to the Pew Research Center analysis. The Center estimates that by 2050 the number of Muslims worldwide will grow to 2.8 billion, or 30% of world's population. Muslims are projected to become the second largest religious group in the U.S., after Christians. By 2050, the American Muslim population is projected to reach 8.1 million people, or 2% of the total population. In contrast, by 2050, European Muslims will make up 10% of the overall population.

Takaful is founded on the cooperative principle of separation between the funds and operations of shareholders and policyholders by passing the ownership of the Takaful (insurance) fund and operations to the policyholders. The policyholders are joint investors with the shareholders (the Takaful operator), who acts as a mudarib (a manager) or an entrepreneurial agent for the policyholders.

Other than the separation of funds, one of other key difference between Takaful and conventional insurance, is that the policyholders, rather than the shareholders, solely benefit from the profits generated from Takaful (insurance) and the invested insurance premiums.

Almost all of the products sold by conventional insurers can also be redesigned to be sold by Takaful operators including auto, marine, health, mortgage reducing Takaful, index linked products, property and many other classes of business.

Bancassurance

SECTION I

THE BRIEF HISTORY OF INSURANCE

Bancassurance is a French term referring to the selling of insurance products through a bank's own distribution channels. The concept first originated in France and soon became popular elsewhere around the world.

Bancassurance takes advantage of the relationship the customer has developed over a period of time with the bank. For an insurance company, selling insurance through the bank is a much more cost effective affair compared to selling through agents. For banks, commission income coming in at a minimum cost is an attractive proposition.

The subject may not be very relevant to the scope of this book considering Bancassurance is frequently used to push individualized products, such as life and auto insurance, rather than commercial insurance products, however, it is such a major operating model that it warrants a mention here.

Understanding The Anatomy of The Insurance Policy

An insurance policy is a contract setting out the terms and conditions of coverage. That is, the Insured pays a premium and the insurer takes on a risk of payment if an event happens.

Many people find difficultly in understand insurance policies because they are inherently complicated. In recent times however, insurance companies have tended towards making their policies as clear as possible in response to courts interpreting any ambiguity in the language against the insurers.

Reading and understanding the insurance policy is necessary to ensure that it provides the needed cover and the Insured is aware of any requirements to comply with its terms and conditions. It must be remembered that claims are paid or rejected in strict compliance with the insurance policy.

SECTION I

UNDERSTANDING THE ANATOMY OF THE INSURANCE POLICY

The main elements of the policy include the Application, Declaration, Definitions, Insuring Agreement, Conditions, Endorsements and Exclusions.

The Application

The application is part of the policy and the Insured must provide all relevant information, failure of which may allow the insurer to void the policy. The information provided at this stage will be used to evaluate the risk and charge the appropriate premium.

The Declaration/ Policy schedule

The declaration page (or the policy schedule), outlines the "Insured", Insured's address, specifies the beginning and end of the policy period (and "retroactive date" may also be stated if a professional liability policy), description and location of the item or items being covered, terms and conditions of coverage, the limits of liability or the total sums insured, any applicable deductibles and the amount of premium.

Definitions

Certain words and phrases appearing throughout the policy document that have particular meaning or have a need for some interpretation will be defined. Such defined words may appear in bold print throughout the policy. For example, "motor vehicle" and "deductible" are two terms often found in an auto policy.

Insuring Agreement/ Coverage

This section describes the outline a broad scope of coverage. This is where the insurance company makes express promises to indemnify the Insured.

Conditions and Warranties

These are a number of provisions, duties and obligations which the Insured must comply with in order for coverage to start, or must remain in compliance with, in order for policy to stay in effect. A common cause for denying policy response is a breach of a condition precedent to liability or policy warranty. For example, a requirement that the Insured provide timely notice to the insurer of all claims and potential claims.

Warranties are another variant of conditions but carry particularly harsh consequences for the Insured if not complied with. Breach of a policy warranty gives the insurer the opportunity to avoid the policy in its entirety, regardless if the breach is relevant to the loss or not and at any time during the policy year. An example would be, "It is warranted that trade waste and wood shavings are swept up and bagged daily and placed in a metal container away from the premises at least once a week." So if this was not complied with and there is a theft of computers, the insurer could void the whole policy and avoid paying for the theft claim. The insurer is discharged from liability even where a warranty has only been breached for a short period of time and the breach has been corrected at the time of a subsequent loss.

Endorsements/Riders

Endorsement and riders are used to tailor the policy by adding optional coverage to the basic policy form, amend any aspect of the interest insured or to clarify certain aspects of the risk and may be subject to additional premium.

Exclusions

Exclusions are listed in insurance policies to define perils, causes of loss or types of damage not covered by the policy. Some of the exclusions can be covered by the insurer on payment of extra premium. For example, flood coverage could have been excluded for businesses located in an area where floods are unlikely to happen. However, the Insured could opt for additional flood cover in return for paying extra premium.

04

Insurance Underwriting Practices and Concepts

The purpose of underwriting is to develop and maintain a profitable business for the insurer. Underwriting is defined as determining what risk will be insured (or refused), for what amount of insurance (the sum insured), at what price (the insurance premium) and under what terms and conditions. Insurance underwriters are professionals that work for insurance companies whose task is to collect appropriate and accurate information to appraise risks, estimate the potential exposure and then make a decision whether or not to accept the application for insurance protecting the insurance company from acquiring non-profitable business.

Insurance Applications/Proposal Forms

The application form is an important part of the documentation of the policy if the proposal is accepted. This document is of particular importance in the case of a claim or any type of dispute that may arise. The application form needs to comply with the legal requirements with respect to discrimination, confidentiality and relevant consumer protection laws. It is a standard document in any legal dispute and as such it should always be legally sound.

Insurance can be sold by an agent, a broker, the government or by mass distribution channels like banks. Depending on the sales channel a different application form will be needed.

Utmost good faith

All insurance contracts rely on the principle of "utmost good faith". This very important principle assumes the presence of mutual faith between the Insured and the insurer.

The Insured must always be honest and accurate in the information they disclose to the insurance company and should not intentionally and knowingly misrepresent facts, give false information or not disclose critical (material) information.

Likewise, the insurance company also has a responsibility to act with good faith in its dealings with the Insured. The insurer for instance should not hide information about the insurance coverage that it is selling or mislead the Insured in to buying a policy.

Misrepresentation and non-disclosure of critical facts

The test for the materiality of a misrepresentation or the willfulness of the Insured is not always so simple to determine, different agencies and regulatory authorities have differing views on what constitutes a material misrepresentation. The law courts have also their share of the action!

In some jurisdictions, a strong argument has been made that an insurer should not be allowed to deny a claim or cancel a policy unless a misrepresentation in the application is both material and was knowingly false, or was made with intent to deceive to the insurer.

This book will consider the potential consequences in the event a misrepresentation was deliberate, the insurer can cancel the policy and deny payment of any claim under that policy.

It is also particularly important to note that whenever a business renews its insurance policy, it is entering into a new contract of insurance. As such, the Insured is required to comply with their duty of disclosure each time the insurance policy is renewed.

Risk assessment

Insurance underwriters will analyze the moral and physical hazards associated with applications that meet the minimum criteria. For example, a commercial property insurance underwriter considers whether the property is in a high-risk flood or earthquake zone. Health insurance underwriters consider medical risks such as pre-existing ailments, family history of cancer or heart disease, or an individual with a history of smoking. Underwriters may communicate with medical doctors, credit bureaus and other agencies to gather additional information as needed.

The risk assessment process may involve others as well, insurance companies have on staff actuaries, engineers and architects in the commercial insurance business and medical doctors in case of the medical and life lines to assist in the study of the information obtained through application forms, third party reports, the internet and physical onsite inspection.

The underwriting decision

Upon the completion of the risk assessment exercise, the underwriter may make anyone of the following decisions based on the underwriting strategy and guidelines of the insurance company:

1. Approve the issuing of a policy by accepting the insurance application at appropriate terms

2. Accept the application but apply additional conditions, restrictions, premium or a combination thereof for coverage

3. Decline the request for coverage

Policy processing

If insurer and Insured are in agreement the application will then be forwarded to the applicable policy processing department for preparation.

05

Policy Deductibles

Deductible can be imposed by the insurer or be voluntarily chosen by the Insured. The higher the deductible amount, the lower the premium payable by the Insured. A higher deductible consequently means that the Insured is contributing more in the event of a claim.

A deductible is defined as the participation of the Insured in a loss up to a certain limit agreed on in advance. A deductible is therefore the amount that the Insured contributes towards a claim. If the amount of the claim is less than the deductible then the Insured does not receive payment at all.

Other names may be used for the deductible, it can also be called an excess. Both terms are used for the same purpose and are often used interchangeably.

Deductibles come in various forms and may be described either in dollar value flat rate deductible, a percentage deductible that is based on the insured value of the

SECTION I

POLICY DEDUCTIBLES

property or a combination deductible that uses a dollar-value deductible in most cases but switches to a percentage based deductible for particular accident scenarios, such as flood related damage. A deductible may also be defined in units of time rather than in dollar value as in the case of most business interruption policies.

Sometimes a deductible type referred to as a Franchise is applied by insurers. A franchise will apply to claims in the same way and for the same reasons as a deductible but in the event that a claim exceeds the franchise the full amount of the loss will be paid.

Certain commercial insurance may apply an Aggregate Deductible. Aggregate deductibles are an amount to be paid by the Insured for all losses sustained during a specific period of time. They are designed to establish a maximum total that an insured is responsible for regardless of the frequency or severity of losses. After the aggregate amount is reached during a single policy year, the Insured no longer participates in future losses, even if they are lower than the per occurrence deductible. Aggregate deductibles are most likely to be features of product liability policies, or policies that may result in a large number of claims during a policy period.

Most disability insurance policies have an Elimination Period deductible or what's called a Waiting Period of one or more months, which stipulates that the Insured be disabled for a time greater than the waiting period. Payments will be made only for the time after the waiting period when the Insured is disabled.

Some policies that have several sections may apply a number of different deductibles to different types of claims.

What purpose do deductibles serve?

Insurers apply deductibles to improve the moral hazard of the Insured hoping that greater interest will be shown in loss prevention and loss reduction since the Insured will have to bear part of the financial burden.

Another important aspect to the insurer is that when a deductible is applied, minor losses will fall under the deductible reducing amount of work and time in accident investigation and settlement therefore reducing administrative expenses.

Increased deductibles are sometimes applied to reflect an increased risk in a certain area of the coverage and it should also be considered that without deductibles, it would be entirely impossible in some cases to cover severe risks.

When businesses consider the size of deductibles in its insurance policies, it has to take into consideration multiple factors. These include, risk severity, risk mitigation measures already in place or under consideration, its historical trend of loss incidences and the insurance marketplace.

Do all policies have deductibles?

No, some types of insurance policies do not have deductibles. For instance, life insurance policies do not have a deductible because a deductible would serve no benefit. A deductible in life insurance would not affect the moral hazard.

Most Liability policies also have no deductible, because almost all liability claims will be for fairly substantial sums of money and because the insurer will want to handle the case from the beginning to minimize legal mistakes that could be more costly later on.

SECTION I

POLICY
DEDUCTIBLES

06

Replacement Value (Cost Value) v Actual Cash Value (Market Value)

These are two distinctly different calculation methods used to determine how much the Insured would receive from the policy to cover an item if it is lost or damaged. The limit on the policy is the most the insurer will pay in the event of a loss or damage. If a constructive total loss of the property insured and the actual replacement costs exceed the limit on the policy the Insured will then be responsible for the difference.

The basis upon which claims for loss or damage to insured property are settled is an important aspect of property, machinery and equipment insurance policies. These policies would specify how assets are valued when lost or damaged. They would also have conditions specifying how the property can be replaced as well as deductions that apply if the property was not insured to its full value.

SECTION I

REPLACEMENT VALUE (COST VALUE) V ACTUAL CASH VALUE (MARKET VALUE)

Although the concepts of market value and actual value are different, both are affected by economic factors. Supply and demand also impacts the (fair) market value. The supply and demand for labor and materials affects replacement cost. When supply does not equal demand, market value, as well as replacement value can quickly change and they can be short term or temporary.

It is important that these valuation methods are properly understood as to what they represent and what factors are considered in each circumstance when limits of insurance are determined and the policy is purchased. The Insured is ultimately responsible for determining the amount of insurance required. Often the help of an appraisal company is recommended and appraisers can be engaged to determine values for insurance purposes.

What is Replacement Value?

Replacement value is a common term used in insurance policies to cover damage to business assets. The insurer agrees to pay the Insured for the replacement cost of covered assets, if those assets are lost or destroyed. The replacement value is the cost of buying or reconstructing or manufacturing a product or asset of equal quality and utility, using prices for labor, materials, overhead, profit and fees in effect at the time of the appraisal to replace a lost or destroyed item. The value is the current cost to replace a lost item on its valuation date.

Replacement cost would not take into consideration improvements necessary to conform to change in building codes, demolition, debris removal, site accessibility, overtime, abnormal soft costs, extraordinary fees and other various contingencies.

Payment based on the replacement is usually the most favorable outcome from the Insured's point of view.

What is Actual cash value?

In contrast, "actual cash value" is the standard that insurance companies prefer in compensating policyholders for their losses.

The term "actual cash value" is not as easily defined or calculated, particular issues may arise after a claim. For example the insurance industry's traditional definition is: the cost to replace with new property of like kind and quality, less depreciation. Some courts have interpreted the term to mean "fair market value" which is the amount a buyer would pay a seller if neither were under undue time constraints. Courts are divided in their rulings as to whether or not depreciation includes obsolescence (loss of usefulness as a result of outmoded design, construction, etc.), these are issues that regularly crop up.

As can be deduced from the description of the two methods, the major difference between "replacement value" and "actual cash value" is the deduction for depreciation. However, both are based on the cost today to replace the damaged property with new property.

What about "Book Value"?

"Book Value" has no relevance to either of the previous methods of valuation. The depreciation rate reflected in "book value" would result in a terribly inadequate claim payout for the policyholder. Another problem with using "book value" is that it may reflect only the items that are "capitalized". This method should be avoided in most cases.

SECTION I

REPLACEMENT VALUE
(COST VALUE) V
ACTUAL CASH VALUE
(MARKET VALUE)

Under-Insurance and The Application of Average

Under-insurance can be defined as the difference between the amount of insurance cover requested at the time a policy is taken out (or when renewed) and the actual cost of replacement or rebuild following a loss such as a cyber-attack, flood or fire and need to make a claim.

It has been reported that 75 percent of commercial buildings in the United States are underinsured by an average of 40 percent or more and that a full 40 percent of businesses may never reopen after a disaster.

In a 2015 study in the United Kingdom, on insurance claims for small and medium sized enterprises, it was reported that there were a significant number of instances where the sum insured was insufficient to cover the loss and in 12 out of the 20 case studies there were issues relating to sums insured. In eight cases the property damage sums insured for buildings, trade contents and or stock were inadequate.

SECTION I

UNDER-INSURANCE AND THE APPLICATION OF AVERAGE

The issue is widespread and perennial. Businesses can be underinsured for many reasons. It appears that if a business has not had a claim before then it can be difficult for owners to see just how much of an impact underinsurance can have on their business.

How can under-insurance arise?

To some customers, deliberate under-insurance can seem like an appealing ploy as it may result in lower premiums but in the event of a claim, this can result in serious financial losses to the Insured, a loss may far exceed any savings made in premium.

Alternatively, instances of under-insurance may arise due to not realizing that items or properties are insured for their market value rather than their reinstatement value. Economic inflation may quickly render the valuation insufficient and so when insurers pay out the market value, the Insured finds that they do not have enough funds to replace the items or properties claimed for.

Business owners may sometimes fail to review their coverage and leave sums insured and indemnity periods untouched for years, despite major changes at their business such as additional employees, new machinery and plant, recent construction or not addressing broader economic factors.

The most common cases of under-insurance are when businesses out of error or omission, do not advise their insurers of additional assets acquired.

In these circumstances, insurers may choose to apply "average" to the claim, resulting in paying out a proportional amount.

What is Average and when is it applied?

Insurers will always seek to receive the correct premium for the risks that they are insuring. Most often, premiums are calculated on a rate applied to the sum insured and insurers will want to see the correct value used as the basis of the premium calculation.

The insurer may choose to apply average if a case of under-insurance at the time of loss has been established, this will mean, any claim will be reduced in the same proportion as the amount of under-insurance that existed at the time of loss. Therefore relieving the insurer and penalizes the Insured for under-insurance.

The application of average is best explained using an example:

Let us assume an office building is insured for USD1,000,000 but actually costs USD2,500,000 to rebuild. The property is only insured for 40% of the sum it should be. Claims will be settled on this basis. If the property suffered water damage of USD20,000, the insurers would only pay a maximum of USD8,000 for the loss. Consequently, the owners are underinsured by USD12,000 and need to cover this amount form own funds. This is the principle of average which applies to most policies.

Personal policies are written with the average private individual and their rather domestic needs in mind, while commercial policies are designed to address the unique needs and situations that arise in commercial use which will be reflected in the premiums charged and the policy conditions.

The Special Condition of Average – 75%

SECTION I

UNDER-INSURANCE AND THE APPLICATION OF AVERAGE

In some cases the insured value may fluctuate so much that it becomes very difficult to determine the exact sum insured.

To avoid average being unfairly applied in these situations some insurers can offer an amended average condition whereby if the sum insured is 75% or more than the value at the time of loss no deduction is made for under-insurance.

"Claims Made" and "Claims Occurring" Policies

In the world of professional liability insurance, insurance cover depends on the type of policy purchased. There are two general types of policies offered: "claims made" and "claims occurring" (sometimes also referred to as "claims arising" or "losses occurring" policies.

A clear understanding of both types of insurance coverage is essential to making a fully informed decision on which type of coverage to purchase. The primary difference between the two is how coverage applies when a claim is made.

"Claims-made" coverage was conceived by professional liability insurers to contain the volatile nature of the "tail". The "tail" in insurance jargon (also called an Extended Reporting Endorsement) refers to both the optional coverage that may be purchased to extend the claims reporting period under a policy and to the length of time between the triggering event (the accident) and the claim. There are exposures that are considered "long tail" and others that are referred to as "short tail".

For example, Asbestosis (a lung disease resulting from prolonged exposure to asbestos), often takes many years to develop, therefore is considered a "long tail" exposure while libel and slander lawsuits resulting from a libelous published article or media broadcast are considered "short tail", because they occur right after the triggering event, i.e. publication.

The reduced insurer liability under "claims made" can mean slightly lower premiums for the Insured. The important thing to understand is why the "claims made" coverage costs less.

Let's dig deeper into the workings of both types of Policies.

The Claims Made Policy

"Claims Made" policies require all and any situation or circumstance, fact or claims, likely to result in a claim to be notified to the insurer within the period of insurance.

The actual mistake could occur at any time where the policy provides unlimited retroactive cover otherwise it must have occurred subsequent to any date specified which limits the retroactive period.

An important issue to note about the "Claims Made" policy is how the coverage and any future claims are impacted if the insurer of the policy is changed. Before changing the insurer, the Insured must make sure that all claims reported in the future for incidents that occurred during the original "Claims Made" policy period are covered. Without continuity, insurers will not provide that all important retroactive coverage.

The following are such examples:

1. The Insured could purchase "tail coverage" on the original "Claims Made" policy. Without tail coverage, claims filed after the "Claims Made" policy expires will not be covered. This will extend the period in which incidents that happened during the initial policy period to be reported and covered.

2. The Insured could purchase "retroactive coverage" from the insurer of the new insurance policy. Retroactive coverage will provide coverage by the new insurer for professional services rendered dating back to a pre-agreed retroactive date. The retroactive date is usually the date the first Professional Liability policy went into effect.

One good advantage of the "Claims Made" policy over the "Occurring Claims" policy is that any accidents that occurred in the past and are claimed now will be paid based on the limits of the current policy, no matter when the incident happened.

Claims Occurring Policy

Occurrence policies are less onerous to understand. An occurrence policy provides coverage for incidents that happened during the policy year regardless of when the claim is reported to the insurer. It provides a separate coverage limit for each year the policy is in force. The policy doesn't have to be active when the claim is reported but the incident has to have happened during its validity.

The main vantage of an occurrence policy is that there is no need to have continuous insurance coverage for a claim to be covered therefore no need to purchase tail or prior acts (retroactive) endorsements in order for past incidents to be covered.

Comparing the Cost

Typically, the annual premium for a "Claims Made" policy costs less than an "Occurrence" policy, sometimes as much as 50%.

The first year of "Claims Made" coverage should typically cost somewhere between 40 and 80% of a "Claims Occurring" policy. But as described earlier, to ensure continued insurance protection after a "Claims Made" policy expires, it's recommended to purchase tail coverage. The additional cost of premiums upfront for a "Claims Occurring" policy, paid at the start of each new policy year, may end up costing more over time than a "Claims Made" policy with tail coverage added on.

The "Claims Made" will involve automatic price increase in subsequent years as the exposure increases. Usually, after three to five years, a "Claims Made" policy is thought to be roughly equivalent to a "Claims Occurring" policy and should cost about the same.

In addition to the cost savings enjoyed in the early years of coverage, in a competitive marketplace Insureds can benefit as underwriters discount the step factors that bring up the price.

If a shift from "Claims Occurring" to "Claims Made" coverage is required, the Insured is best advised to seek professional legal advice to revise any employment contracts, partnership agreements and other similar contracts to specify who will be responsible for buying tail coverage.

Supplementing Insurance Coverage

*"Difference in Conditions" and "Difference in Limits"
(DIC and DIL) Policies*

This supplementary cover is sometimes required by businesses that have operations located in different countries and insured locally. Businesses face increasingly complicated country laws and regulations and may have most of their risks insured locally in that territory. It sometimes happens that the cover provided by the locally issued policies may not provide the same level of cover as the primary insurance policy of the business as certain covers or limits may not be locally available. The business may as a result be exposed to losses in certain territories with more restricted cover or with lower limits than they would be under their main insurance policy. A DIC or DIL cover would provide a uniform level of cover and limits for their international insurance programs.

There is no standard DIC or DIL coverage form or wording and insurers will draft their own forms.

SECTION I

SUPPLEMENTING INSURANCE COVERAGE

How is a "Difference in Conditions" policy used?

A DIC policy allows coverage to be customized to extend cover according to the Insured's needs. The policy is designed to broaden provided coverage for perils that are excluded on basic coverage policy.

DIC coverage may be provided by way of a separate insurance policy or it may be added by endorsement to the existing basic policy.

How is a "Difference in Limits" policy used?

The DIL policy would provide additional limits of coverage for specific perils when standard markets won't provide adequate limits of coverage.

This difference in limits allows the cover to "trickle down" to supplement any limits on a locally arranged insurance policy in order to provide the same limits as the primary insurance policy. DIL coverage may also be provided by way of a separate insurance policy or it may be added by endorsement to the existing basic policy.

THE INSURANCE
FIELD BOOK

Secion 2

Insurance Policy Coverage Explained

SECTION 2

THE COMMERCIAL
AUTO INSURANCE
POLICY

The Commercial Auto Insurance Policy

(Motor Fleet Comprehensive Insurance)

Accident reports in the news frequently focus on spectacular road accidents such as overturned fuel tankers or fatal collisions involving multiple vehicles in atrocious weather conditions. Accidents involving commercial vehicles are no doubt more serious because of their size and carrying weight resulting in expensive damage and serious injuries in contrast to accidents involving smaller and lighter vehicles.

Needless to say, business owners need to prepare for every situation to protect their investment in the vehicles that they use and also to protect them against potential liabilities towards others. Despite the best efforts of motor fleet managers, road conditions, weather and other drivers are out of their control.

SECTION 2

THE COMMERCIAL AUTO INSURANCE POLICY

Liability insurance is the most basic cover for motorized vehicles used on public roads and is a mandatory requirement in most countries around the world.

Law, regulation and practice do differ from one country to another and also from one state to another in auto insurance in particular, therefore the information in this section must be used for general guidance only.

Who is the policy suitable for?

Commercial vehicle insurance is needed to cover the cars, pickup trucks, lorries, trailers, vans, buses and other motorized vehicles driven on public roads and used by the Insured or their employees in conducting business activities.

Large fleet operators, as well as small businesses, can be covered by a commercial auto insurance policy. Operators of buses, taxis, rental cars, construction equipment (driven under own power on public roads), courier motorbike fleets and such like are examples of the typical commercial policyholder.

Cover description

Universally speaking, a commercial auto insurance policy includes the following two types of basic covers:

- **Third party liability**
    - » Provides cover for bodily injury, death and property damage to others resulting from an accident for which the Insured or his employee is at fault.
    - » The policy may include a combined single limit per occurrence for bodily injury and property damage (an

occurrence may involve more than one person and several properties in a single accident). In most countries, the minimum limit of liability provided under a motor insurance policy is determined by law and regulations.

- **Comprehensive and collision damage (damage to own vehicle)**

    » Provides cover for damage to the Insured's vehicle from events such as:
    » theft, vandalism, falling objects, fire, cracked windshield glass, earthquake, hailstorm and flood (note that insuring against natural perils may entail additional cost)
    » collision events regardless of who is at fault.

What does it pay for?

A commercial auto policy will protect against the cost of repairing any property damaged belonging to others, the medical bills resulting from injuries to others and pays compensation if a third party is killed. Additionally, reimbursement for expenses of defending legal action if another party in the accident files a lawsuit against the Insured and pays the resulting damages awarded by the court.

Collision coverage will pay for the cost of repairs to the vehicle insured or if it is considered a total loss, will pay a certain amount towards the replacement of the insured vehicle.

SECTION 2

THE COMMERCIAL AUTO INSURANCE POLICY

Possible policy extensions

A commercial auto policy may be extended to include cover for acts of nature (for example flood, storm, hail, earthquake or tsunami), medical expenses of the driver and passengers (referred to as Personal Injury Protection), blanket additional Insured, personal effects cover, lease and loan gap cover, injuries and damages caused by an uninsured or a hit and run driver, damage to others during loading and unloading, vehicles the Insured had leased or hired or rented or borrowed for incidental usage in business, car rental reimbursement or temporary replacement vehicle for covered damage, towing and labour, custom parts or accessories cover such as audio and video equipment and personal accident benefits against death or disability to driver and passengers.

Extending policy coverage will entail additional premium charges.

General exclusions

Auto policies share a standard list of policy exclusions that would include (but not limited to) loss, damage or expense due to:

- driver being below a certain age
- intentional acts, partaking in racing or trial events
- not possessing valid and current licence or appropriate licence for the type of vehicle
- being under the influence of alcohol or drugs
- radioactive contamination, chemical, biological, electromagnetic weapons, war, invasion, strike, riot or civil commotion and terrorism risks.

Other notable examples of excluded risks include:

- vehicle carrying more passengers than it's designed for
- vehicle not being roadworthy and loss
- damage due to natural calamities

A monetary deductible for each and every loss occurring to the insured vehicle will be applicable.

Setting the sum insured and the liability limit

For the *third party liability* section of the policy, the minimum limit of liability for third party damage or injury is usually specified by law or regulations. However, the Insured in some instances may request higher limits of indemnity which the insurer may entertain in return for additional premium.

For the *comprehensive and collision* section of the policy, the purchase price for a brand new vehicle will be the insured value, while for others, the insured value is the market value of the vehicle.

Market practice is to provide cover on market-value basis, however, there may be instances where the insurer agrees to cover used vehicles on an agreed-value basis in return for additional premium.

Policy premium calculation

Premium reduction offers can be made to businesses that have put together a package of measures which will convince an insurer that future risk will be lower, such measures must be capable of improving the claims experience.

For example, making employees aware that the management team monitors accidents and will take action

SECTION 2

THE COMMERCIAL AUTO INSURANCE POLICY

where needed, retraining drivers if necessary, reducing reliance on young drivers aged 17-20 and providing good vehicle security.

To calculate the annual premium for an auto insurance policy, a premium rate per one hundred dollar will be multiplied by the total sum insured of all vehicles in the fleet to arrive at the policy premium.

What information do the insurers need to be told in an insurance application?

Insurers usually have underwriting information requirement that is usually quite extensive and will include information relating to types of vehicle and trailers composing the fleet, business use of vehicles and the territories in which they operate, market value for each vehicle, age of vehicles, parking and security while vehicles are idle and claims history for at least the last 3 years.

It is usual practice for the Insured to indicate the excess that is desired for any claims incurred considering the high frequency of claims expected under this policy. The magnitude of the excess will have a big impact on the insurers offered premium.

A COMMON MISCONCEPTION

Many self-employed individuals believe that their personal car insurance policy covers them for work and business use!

Unfortunately, when time comes to file a claim that belief might not stand up to scrutiny and the insurer may reject the claim. Insurance companies consider commercial auto insurance and personal car insurance to be two very different types of policies due to the differences in risk and liability.

Personal policies are written with the average private individual and their rather domestic needs in mind, while commercial policies are designed to address the unique needs and situations that arise in commercial use which will be reflected in the premiums charged and the policy conditions.

Recent research findings and developing trends on driver behavior and accident causes

Recent research on driving habits in the USA revealed that engaging in visual and manual subtasks, such as reaching for a phone, dialling and texting associated with the use of mobile phones and other portable devices while driving, increased the risk of being involved in a crash by three times. Statistics gathered in 2014 has shown that 3,179people were killed in motor vehicle crashes involving distracted drivers. This represents an increase from 1.7 to 2.2 per cent in the number of drivers text-messaging or visibly manipulating handheld devices. Unfortunately, approximately 431,000 people were injured, which is an increase from the 424,000 people that were injured in 2013.

Moreover, drivers in their 20s make up 27 per cent of the distracted drivers in fatal crashes.

In the UK, a 2003 study has found that up to 30 per cent of all traffic accidents are work related. While a Euro zone study has found the main causes of truck accidents on the road are linked to human error (85%) while other factors such as weather, road conditions or mechanical failure played a minor role.

Citing findings of another survey in the UK, drivers of company cars especially those of vans, pickups and lorries, were more likely than drivers of non-company cars to drive:

- Under pressure of time
- While being tired
- While being distracted by demanding tasks

In fact, drivers of company cars viewed speeding as a casual factor, van drivers showed observational failures and lorry crashes were closely related to fatigue and vehicle defects.

Case Studies

The following claims scenarios highlight the range of potential accidents that could arise in the normal course of business.

CASE 1: A sale manager was making sales call to a customer while driving his car during the evening rush hour. He collided with another car badly denting his car. The driver in the other car suffered whiplash injury and damages to the back of his car.

CASE 2: The driver of a tanker lorry carrying flammable liquefied petroleum gas (LPG) struck a roadside barrier whilst trying to avoid another vehicle. The lorry rolled over and settled on its side, the gas caught fire resulting in an explosion destroying the lorry, killing its driver and damaging 7 others vehicles.

CASE 3: A large company van used to deliver flowers was heavily damaged during a hail storm. The hailstones, some of them as big as baseballs, smashed windows, injured people and caused traffic chaos. The hail was accompanied by ferocious winds in excess of 75 mph.

Useful reading

Official U.S. Government website for Distracted Driving.

SECTION 2

THE COMMERCIAL
AUTO INSURANCE
POLICY

The Burglary Insurance Policy

Every business possessing valuable property that has a market value and is readily resalable is subject to attack by burglars. The greater the value of this property, the greater is the possibility of loss.

When small businesses become victims of crime, they often react by raising their prices to cover their losses, changing their hours of work, relocating to another area or simply closing permanently. Business closures due to crime could have an impact on other local businesses.

The impact of crime on business can be widespread and includes lost revenue for the government, fear of job loss by employees and higher insurance premiums.

Who is the policy suitable for?

This policy can be purchased by businesses of any size and occupation holding valuable property, for instance, stock-in-trade, furniture, fixtures, goods held in trust or on commission, portable machinery and tools, designs, patterns and moulds and office equipment of every description.

Cover description

This policy covers loss of or damage to contents whilst contained in the specified business or trade premises arising from:

- Theft consequent upon actual forcible and violent entry into the premises such as picking a lock, breaking a window, or slashing a screen
- Theft or any attempted theft by a person feloniously concealed in the said premises
- Damage to the property insured or premises due to theft or attempted burglary
- Hold-up or armed robbery

What does it pay for?

The policy compensates the Insured for the value of the contents lost or damaged in addition to the associated cost of repair to premises if damaged during the forceful entry or exit from premises.

Possible policy extensions

Most commonly requested extensions to the burglary policy include cover for riot, strike, civil commotion, malicious damage, loss or damage to the property of employees and also expenses towards clean-up of debris.

Adding these extensions to the policy cover will entail additional premium charges.

General exclusions

The policy will not pay for loss or damage to jewelry, gold, cash, bonds plans, designs, money, deeds, shop lifting, unexplained or mysterious disappearances, war, riots, strikes and civil commotion, acts of god and nuclear perils.

A deductible for each and every loss may be applicable under the policy.

Setting the sum insured

The sum insured can be fixed either on First Loss Basis or on Full Value Basis, the former being the most common method for setting the sum insured under a burglary policy. This would be the maximum that the insurer would be expected to pay in compensation.

1. **First Loss Basis**
   This basis is adopted when it is not possible for the entire property insured to be stolen at the same time. The sum insured shall be based on Insured's assessment.

2. **Full Value Basis**
   This basis is adopted when there exists a possibility of the entire property insured being stolen at any one time. The Insured must ensure adequacy of the sum insured. The correct sum insured should be what the Insured considers to be the highest value at risk at any one time.

Policy premium calculation

Improving the security features of the premises by making sure all access points to premises are secure, having a well maintained burglar alarm system and high quality

SECTION 2

THE BURGLARY INSURANCE POLICY

security locks on windows and doors could help to lower the premium rates as it reduces the risk of claims occurring.

The insurers will pay particular attention to concentration of value in items that may be stolen and easily converted to cash. Of equal importance would be the area the business is located in which may be classified as high risk if for instance, crimes are wide spread especially burglaries.

A premium rate per one thousand dollar will be multiplied by the sum insured deduced by either of the methods mentioned above to arrive at the annual policy premium.

What information do the insurers need to be told in an insurance application?

Burglary coverage is usually included in a fire or a property all risks policy, therefore most of the required information would have been collected in a fire proposal. Therefore, a separate burglary proposal form is seldom needed.

In the event that a separate proposal is needed such would contain questions relating to past accident experience, building type, business hours, itemized list of contents, the intruder detection system and security policy used in the protection of premises during and after office hours.

A COMMON MISCONCEPTION

Theft, robbery and burglary are different names for the same act!

This couldn't be further from the truth, in fact, legally, consequences range from the severe to the moderate but they are all nonetheless punishable crimes. From an insurance perspective, the burglary definition used in most insurance policies is the unlawful taking of property from within premises, entry to which has been obtained by force, leaving visible marks of entry.

However, from a legal perspective, according to the US legal system, a burglary is committed when a person enters a building or a structure illegally or without authorization, any type of force used (no matter how minimal would satisfy the break-in requirement), additionally, the judge must be convinced that the defendant entered with the intention to commit a felony or a theft, even if nothing was stolen. Depending on the jurisdiction, the sentence could reach up to 20 years in prison and/or up to USD100,000 in fines. The definitions of theft and robbery are beyond the scope of this book but the reader may consult law books for additional information.

Recent research findings and developing trends relating to crime against business

The total cost of crime to business is difficult to measure and may never be fully calculated. According to the U.S. Chamber of Commerce, crime may be a factor in as many as 30 per cent of all business failures. Small businesses may be particularly vulnerable to crime as small businesses often do not have safeguards in place to prevent and detect criminal activity.

Commercial establishments have certain appealing characteristics that may heighten their vulnerability to burglary. Offenders prefer a lower concentration of businesses and traffic and shy away from major intersections or highly patrolled areas. Businesses located on corners have a higher risk of burglary as they offer multiple directions for escape. The types of businesses with the highest

SECTION 2

THE BURGLARY INSURANCE POLICY

burglary rates are office park suites, retail establishments, and single office buildings.

According to the *Crime in the United States* (CIUS) 2007 report, stolen office equipment alone totaled a staggering USD657million.

Case Studies

The following claims scenarios highlight the range of potential accidents that could arise in the normal course of business.

CASE 1: A security guard was hit on the head and fell unconscious after challenging burglars who had broken into the premises of an electronic consumer goods distributor during the night. A truck load of flat screen TVs' were stolen with cost estimated at USD500,000. The police were able to arrest the suspects within 4 days however only 20% of the stolen goods were recovered.

CASE 2: Thieves broke into an office of architects and stole expensive computer equipment and accessories. Surveillance cameras captured two men walking across the parking garage to a door and prying it open. The men were seen leaving about 10 minutes later, each carrying several items.

CASE 3: An estimated USD 6,000 worth of merchandise was stolen from an eyewear shop after two masked suspects were caught on surveillance cameras using a brick to shatter a store window. The shop owner discovered the incident when she came to open the store the following morning.

The Business Interruption Insurance Policy

(Consequential Loss / Increased Cost of Working)

There is growing realization that significant loss of income presents more of a threat than the loss or destruction of property and plant. Ever greater interconnectivity between businesses means a fire or a flood at a manufacturing business in one region can cause a knock on business interruption elsewhere, not just for the business itself but also for other businesses unable to operate because of the effect on a supplier, in this case the manufacturer.

Leaner supply practices in manufacturing and intensive use of computing made business operations more vulnerable and created substantially higher business interruption risks.

When a business suffers a property loss from a fire, theft or storm, it may be forced to suspend business or move to a new location on temporary or permanent basis. But the reality is that, even when the business is closed, it still

SECTION 2

THE BUSINESS
INTERRUPTION
INSURANCE POLICY

must pay bills, rent or mortgage payments, taxes, bank loans, suppliers and others. The company may also have to incur additional expenses related to the loss, such as employee overtime, moving and storage expenses and rent for a temporary location.

Preserving earnings power is one of the main priorities that any business manager must have.

Who is the policy suitable for?

Business interruption represents huge exposures for manufacturing industries as well as businesses in the services industry.

Business that has to close down completely while the premises are being repaired may lose out to competitors therefore this type of policy is almost universally required by businesses of all kinds and sizes.

Cover description

In practice, business interruption policies include a *material damage proviso* meaning that the interruption to business has to result from an insurable physical damage to the insured property.

This physical loss or damage has to have been covered under another policy that is in force, the following are common examples:

- Loss or damage caused to the premises under a Fire insurance policy by fire, storm, flooding and other insured perils, or,
- The accidental breakdown of plant or machinery under a Machinery Breakdown insurance policy

The policy will provide cover from the date of the physical loss and extends to when the business turnover and profit levels are back to where they would have been before the loss subject to a maximum period of time referred to as the Indemnity Period.

There are, typically, three types of these policies, a policy may also consist of only one or a combination of all three, so make sure the policy wording is checked carefully:

1. **Business Interruption**, where policy covers the loss of revenue the business has suffered following physical loss or damage

2. **Increased Cost of Working (ICOW)**, this is where policy covers only the additional expenses that the business has incurred in ensuring the continuity of operation following physical loss or damage

3. **Contingent Loss of Profit**, this protects the Insured when physical loss or damage occurs at a key supplier's or customer's premises causing loss of revenue for the Insured

What does it pay for?

The insurance payout will enable the Insured to recoup financial losses incurred from the loss of revenue, loss of rental income, supplier costs, increased cost of working, continuing expenses (payments for staff salaries, loan repayments, taxes etc.) to make up for the difference between business' normal income and its income during and immediately after a forced shutdown enabling the Insured to maintain cash flow while equipment is being replaced and physical damage to their property is repaired.

Possible policy extensions

Insurance cover can be extended to include increased cost of working (ICOW) and contingent loss of profit, prevention or denial of access, closure by public authority, outstanding debt balances due to loss of records, claims preparation costs and professional accountant fees.

It's interesting to note, that policies for hotels and restaurants can be extended to cover interruption due to murder, suicide and contagious disease.

Adding additional coverage to the policy will entail additional premium charges.

General exclusions

The policy will include various exclusions including but not limited to loss or damage due to war and war like operations, radioactive contamination or nuclear perils, pollution or contamination, electrical or mechanical breakdown, burglary, wear and tear, seepage, pollution and contamination.

Insurers like to include a deductible in the form of a waiting period which must elapse before any loss is payable, typically ranging from the first 3 to the first 21 days.

Setting the sum insured and the indemnity period

Deciding the sum insured for a business interruption policy is probably one of most difficult tasks for the average Insured. The calculation of the sum insured gets even more complicated for a new or a growing small business.

In addition to calculating the sum insured, the business owner must also decide on the period that would be required to restore business turnover to the level that it was just before the loss i.e. the *Indemnity Period*. This is a period cap, for example 12 months, for which the loss will continue to be compensated for by the insurer.

The advice and assistance of a qualified professional broker is highly recommended in deciding the sum insured and the indemnity period.

We will set out below in simple terms the generalized requirements of two different methods for calculating the sum insured:

Method 1

1. Calculate the projected turnover for the following year taking into account opening and closing balance of stock and include an estimate of payroll that the business will maintain taking into account that this may be reduced by eliminating casual labor, redundancies etc.

2. Estimate the costs that can be reduced or eliminated in the event of a loss

The sum insured is calculated by deducting item 2 from the estimated annual turnover. This is the most common method used since costs that were not deducted in the calculation are automatically insured.

Method 2

1. Calculate the projected net profit for the following year without deducting income taxes

2. Calculate the projected fixed expenses which will continue to be payable even if the business has come to a halt, this may include the following items:

- Bank interest charges
- Taxes
- Rent
- Advertising
- Salaries and wages
- Heat, light, water, internet and telephone expenses

By adding the total of the two headings listed above a figure will be reached for the sum insured of business interruption.

It is advisable that an estimate for the additional expenses which the business may incur to enable it continue its operation following the accident (ICOW) is also included, for example:

- Temporary office premises
- Moving expenses
- Equipment rental
- Additional salaries
- Additional expenses to accountants or lawyers

Policy premium calculation

A business that tries to mitigate the impact of sustaining large losses by taking the necessary loss prevention measures, putting in place a robust business continuity plan and has data backup facility in secure offsite location will definitely allow it to benefit from lower premium rates from insurers.

A premium rate per one thousand dollar of the sum insured will be multiplied by the estimated total sum insured arrived at using either of the methods mentioned above to arrive at the annual policy premium.

What information do the insurers need to be told in an insurance application?

Insurers will need to gather certain information to satisfy their underwriting requirement and this will include questions relating to contingency planning, bottlenecks, internal backup alternatives, redundancies in operating (for example, machinery not running at full capacity), workforce and their flexibility regarding overtime and location, repair times for machinery and restoration time for buildings and availability of similar businesses nearby for outsourcing.

The extent of policy coverage and past claims history for existing fire or machinery breakdown policies and the susceptibility to natural or man-made damage will be assessed to give better understanding of the associated risks.

Insurers will pay special attention to the method in which the Insured has calculated the necessary sum insured for the sake of preventing future issues arising in the definition of insurance-gross-profit and expected values, if a claim arises (remember that the gross profit calculated for insurance purposes is different from accounting gross profit as has been explained earlier).

A COMMON MISCONCEPTION

Employees can collect unemployment benefits in the event of stoppage to business, so no need to include salaries and wages in the business interruption policy!

An employee should not be required to claim unemployment benefits if their employer cannot pay them because of a covered business interruption loss.

SECTION 2

THE BUSINESS
INTERRUPTION
INSURANCE POLICY

> Moreover, it is less disruptive for the employer to continue paying the employee through the business interruption policy during the time it takes to get the business up and running therefore, keeping hold of staff that would otherwise join competitors.

Recent research findings and developing trends on business interruption risks

Business interruption ranks as the top concern of businesses in 2016 for the fourth year in succession rating this as one of the three most important risks for companies alongside market developments risk and cyber risk. It is expected that sizable financial losses in the future will result from events such as cyber incidents and technical failures, interruptions caused by import and export restrictions, disrupted production due to strikes, political violence, terrorism, war or the actions of authorities and loss of reputation due to various environmental, social and governance activities.

Catastrophes caused by supernatural disasters such as floods, tsunamis, volcanic eruptions, wildfires and others represent major threats and create significant losses to property and more so than ever in business interruption with far reaching repercussions throughout the economic system, interrupting supply chains and global travel.

In a study published in the US in 2007, it was estimated that 25 per cent of those businesses that closedown following events such as these do not reopen and many that do, struggle to stay in business.

Case Studies

The following claims scenarios highlight the range of potential accidents that could arise in the normal course of business.

CASE 1: A severe winter snowstorm caused a week-long power failure shutting down an e-commerce website selling fashion garments. The melting snow had also endangered thousands of dollars' worth of inventory stored in a basement. The business, to ensure continuity additionally had to pay for storage and relocation costs.

CASE 2: A glass manufacturer whose factory is powered by natural gas received through a pipeline coming from a natural gas production plant had production halted when an explosion rocked the plant. Plant reconstruction and commissioning will take more than 2 years and the manufacturer has to find an alternative source of natural gas.

CASE 3: A small family printing business involved also in publishing and banner making had all of its desktop computers and laptops stolen. The business ground to a halt until new computers were purchased and configured with the necessary software and myriad of device drivers to reconnect the new computers with the printing machines. This meant a complete stoppage for almost two week.

SECTION 2

THE BUSINESS
INTERRUPTION
INSURANCE POLICY

The Marine Cargo Insurance Policy

Many businesses use carriers and freight forwarding companies for transporting goods to and from specified locations, customs clearance processing and storage. While electronic communications and faster travel times have made the relative distance between regions of the world appear much smaller, the physical separation of these same regions is still a very important reality. The greater the physical separation, the more likely freight can be damaged in one of the transport operations involved.

The liability of the various cargo service providers such as carriers and freight forwarders is, as a general rule, very limited in the event the cargo is lost, damaged or delayed and may in some cases be wholly absent as in act of god incidents.

The variety of goods being shipped is infinite, from the transportation of brand new motor vehicles in RORO ferries and unpackaged barley grains in ocean going bulk carriers to the daily transportation of fresh salmon by airplanes across far distant continents. Some can be damaged by impact while others can be damaged by unexpected temperature variations.

SECTION 2

THE MARINE CARGO INSURANCE POLICY

Marine cargo insurance continues to play an important role in domestic and international trade in relieving traders, manufacturers and others of the some of the financial burden involved when goods are lost or damaged during shipping.

Who is this policy suitable for?

Most contracts of sale require that goods be insured either by the seller or the buyer against loss or damage. The policy can be arranged by businesses that typically import materials or stock from abroad, or those that export goods overseas, whether a manufacturer, supplier, wholesaler, retailer or cargo agent and be it transported by rail, road, sea or air.

INCOTERMS define the responsibilities of the seller and buyer and are used to determine the extent of insurable interest in each shipment. Responsibility for loss or damage to goods in transit is assigned to the seller, the buyer or both for a portion or all of the transit. (*INCOTERMS* are internationally recognized trade terms published by the International Chamber of Commerce that apply primarily to international trade, not domestic trade).

Cover description

The marine cargo insurance policy is universal in the sense that the practice followed by the insurers is more or less internationally uniform and reflects the principles and practices prevailing in the London market or Lloyd's. (There are exceptions however, for instance the American market uses clauses developed by the American Institute of Marine Underwriters (AIMU) which are considered similar to the ICC clauses with certain adaptations relevant to the US).

Coverage can be on the basis of one of the following internationally recognised clauses, commonly known as Institute Cargo Clauses (ICC). These are updated every now and then and it may be noticed that insurance policies regularly make reference to 1/1/82 and 1/1/09 clauses, the dates refer to updates, the last of which is that of 2009.

Typically, cover starts from the time the goods leave the premises and terminates upon delivery of goods, to the final destination or 60 days after discharge from the vessel for sea cargo and 30 days after landing for air cargo, whichever shall occur first.

Institute Cargo Clauses A (ICC A) – generally referred to as all risks cover

Covers all risks of loss of or damage to the goods insured except as excluded under the policy. Generally, cover would allow for the following perils:

- Theft, pilferage and non-delivery
- Rough handling
- Piracy

Perils covered under ICC B & ICC C
Institute Cargo Clauses B (ICC B)

Includes perils covered under ICC C (see below) plus the following:

- Earthquake, volcanic eruption or lightning
- Washing overboard
- Entry of sea, lake or river water into vessel, craft, hold, conveyance, container, lift van or place of storage

- Total loss of package lost overboard or dropped whilst loading on to or unloading from vessel or craft

Institute Cargo Clauses C (ICC C)

- Fire or explosion
- Vessel or craft being stranded, grounded, sunk or capsized
- Overturning or derailment of land conveyance
- Collision or contact of vessel, craft or conveyance with external object other than water
- Discharge of cargo at a port of distress
- General average sacrifice
- Jettison

Institute Cargo Clauses (Air)

These are identical to the all risks clauses ICC (A) but adapted to air rather than sea voyages.

In addition to the universal use of the A, B and C clauses, certain trade associations have negotiated adaptations to these clauses relating to frozen foods, coal, bulk oil, commodity trades, jute, natural rubber, oils, seeds, fats, frozen meat and timber industries placing more emphasis on the unique features of each trade.

A cover that is commonly provided by the policy is what is known as **General Average,** which is a loss arising through a voluntary sacrifice of any part of the ship or its cargo, or expenditure to safeguard the ship and the rest of its cargo. When the vessel owner declares a general average, it will result in that all the cargo interests and the vessel owner share the expenses associated with the general average proportionately. Such losses can be significant and may require letters of guarantee to have the cargo released.

Generally, these expenses are covered under the marine cargo policy. A letter of guarantee would be issued by the cargo insurers and is an agreement to meet the Insured's liability for contribution.

Typically insurance policies can take one of the following forms:

- **Single voyage policy**

    the most common type of policy and it covers cargo when it's shipped from one place to another in one voyage.

- **Marine open cover policy**

    an open policy is the agreement between the Insured and the insurance company to insure all cargos in transit falling within that agreement for an indefinite period or until the agreement is cancelled by either party. Insurance certificates are issued once shipments are declared as evidence of contract.

- **Annual policy**

    an annual policy is to cover risks for a period of time, usually one year and all the shipments should fall within the terms and conditions of the policy. Again insurance certificates are issued once shipments are declared.

What does it pay for?

The policy usually provides protection against the actual costs of replacing goods lost or damaged during shipping or while kept in warehousing in the interim period, the costs incurred in trying to minimize loss, general average contribution and expenses involved in inspection.

Possible policy extensions

This policy may be extended to include loss or damage due to war, strikes, riots, civil commotions, terrorism, removal of debris, container demurrage charges, cost of re-consignment or re-shipping, liability for loss or damage to container and delayed unpacking.

Adding additional perils and extending the policy coverage will entail additional premium charges.

General exclusions

There is widely accepted list of excluded perils that excludes all loss, damage or expense attributable to the willful misconduct of the Insured, inherent vice or nature of insured items, ordinary leakage, loss in weight or volume or wear and tear of insured items, insolvency or financial default of the owners, managers, charterers or operators of the vessel, un-seaworthiness or unfitness of vessel or craft, conveyance, insufficiency or unsuitability of packing or preparation of the insured items, delay even though the delay is caused by a risk insured against, any weapon of war or any weapon employing atomic or nuclear fission or fusion or other like reaction or radioactive force or matter, war, strikes, riots and civil commotions.

A deductible for each and every loss under the policy may be applicable under the policy.

Setting the sum insured

The sum insured or value of the policy would depend upon the type of contract of sale agreed between buyer and seller. Normally, in addition to the invoice value a 10 to 20% is added on top to cover incidental costs or expenses and profit margin.

The most common contracts are:

- Free on Board or FOB
- Cost and Freight or C&F
- Cost, Insurance and Freight or CIF

In FOB and C&F contracts, the buyer is responsible for purchasing the insurance policy. In CIF contracts, the seller is responsible for insurance from his own premises to that of the purchaser's.

Typically, both the open cover and the annual policy will apply a pre-agreed maximum limit for insured value per any one consignment or vehicle or ship or other conveyance. The insurance company will have to price in advance any shipment exceeding this limit on case by case basis.

Policy premium calculation

Premium rates vary depending on the method of shipping, method of packing, the specific voyage, route used and the nature of the cargo shipped. Naturally, goods that are susceptible to loss or damage, for example fragile or attractive for theft, would attract higher rates.

Businesses can control their claims experience thereby influencing the rates they are charged by addressing loss prevention, cargo security and the logistics chain to identify areas of vulnerability and to apply any needed improvements.

A premium rate per one hundred dollar will be multiplied by the estimated annual shipments to arrive at the provisional annual policy premium.

It is usual practice for the insurer to provide a schedule of marine rates for an open cargo policy which can be used by the Insured to calculate the cost of insurance on each type of cargo.

What information do the insurers need to be told in an insurance application?

The underwriters will require information on the desired scope of coverage, extra expenses percentage, estimated volume of annual shipments, destinations or ports, estimated values of sea and air shipments, estimated values of imports and exports, shipping routes, the age and ownership of carrying vessel, length of voyage, packing arrangements and past claims experience.

Of equal importance will be information on the susceptibility of the goods to damage, theft and pilferage.

A COMMON MISCONCEPTION

We don't need cargo Insurance because the carrier must be insuring our goods!

This could prove to be a fatal mistake. Carriers' conditions of carriage protect the carrier not the owner of goods. Liability is usually limited by weight and cover for loss or damage is only provided whilst the goods are in the carriers' custody and they usually exclude liability for circumstances beyond the carriers' control or where loss is due to fire, explosion, vessel being grounded, capsized, sunk or when container falls overboard. If the carrier is not negligent then their policy will probably not respond to a claim.

The Insured should check the conditions of carriage to see if they are adequate for their needs.

Recent research findings and developing trends on major causes of losses

It is commonly reported that road collisions rank at top of the list of the most frequent accident causes. Cargo transported across national borders by trucks is frequently involved in bad weather collisions with other vehicles. Theft of cargo and fire are the next costliest loss causes. Theft of expensive metals such as copper, feature in many of the accidents reported because of its high value and the fact that it is used in many industries such as electric cable making and in steel manufacturing.

Natural catastrophes can destroy cargo just as they do to property, some have contributed to some of the largest marine cargo losses ever recorded. Super storm Sandy in 2012, Tohuku (Japan) earthquake and tsunami in 2011 and floods in Thailand in 2011 are examples from recent memory.

Losses due to piracy of cargo ships for increasingly larger ransom demands indicates pirates gained knowledge of the values of cargos and ships. The decreasing value of ships has in many instances meant that the value of cargo is larger than that of the carrying vessel.

SECTION 2

Case Studies

THE MARINE CARGO
INSURANCE POLICY

The following claims scenarios highlight the range of potential accidents that could arise in the normal course of business.

CASE 1: The cargo stowed on a vessel crossing the ocean is tossed violently as a gigantic tidal wave caused by an earthquake under the seabed buffeted the ship. The cargo was severely damaged.

CASE 2: A heavy truck trailer fully laden with brand new stock of smart phones travelling from USA to Canada swerves off the road in icy conditions and plunges into a river killing its driver and rendering the cargo worthless.

CASE 3: In the early morning's thick fog, RoRo-vessel, the Tricolor on its way from Zeebrugge to Southampton, carrying almost 3,000 BMWs, Volvos and Saabs, collided with a container ship named Kariba, in the English Channel. Approximately 2,862 cars were lost.

14

The Carrier's Liability Insurance Policy

(Hauliers Liability insurance)

Most businesses have some requirement for transporting products and expect carriers-for-hire to deliver their goods to the correct destination, without damage and on time. These businesses have come to rely on freight forwarding companies for transporting goods to and from specified locations.

Professional transport companies shift thousands of products between customers and therefore are liable for loss or damage to goods while they are being transported regardless of cause in most cases. Where goods are lost or damaged, it is possible that someone, during the transportation, has been negligent. If there has been negligence, there is likely to be a demand for compensation.

There are basically four types of contracts of carriage used universally between goods carrier/forwarder and the goods owner, each determining the responsibility for loss or damage to goods and the extent of that responsibility. Briefly, these are:

1. **Limited Carriers Risk**
   Carriers liability is limited to amounts per unit of goods as stipulated under certain acts or laws or regulation in force in that particular country or state. The amount is in most cases nominal and could range from few hundred dollars to few thousands, again depending on that country or state. The majority of goods are carried under these terms.

2. **Declared Value**
   The carrier will be liable for an amount agreed between carrier and owner up to that specified in the contract of carriage. Used regularly for containerized goods.

3. **Declared Terms**
   The carrier will be liable under terms and conditions of the contract agreed between carrier and owner. Extraordinary features of the goods or the route may dictate the terms of this contract.

4. **Owners Risk**
   The carrier will not be liable for loss or damage at all. Most commonly used for furniture and office removals.

Who is the policy suitable for?

A Carriers Liability policy is recommended for businesses involved in transporting goods belonging to others under contract such as movers, haulers and couriers, using trucks, vans, rail or other means from the supplier of goods to the buyer or end recipient.

This policy should not to be purchased by owners or prospective owners of the goods being transported and as such a Marine Cargo or an Inland Transit policy would be more suitable in their case.

Cover description

The policy covers the legal liability of the carrier for damage to goods the carrier was contracted to carry in transit including loading and unloading and whilst temporarily stored on or off vehicles.

Liability limit may be subject to the provisions of carriage of goods acts or government regulations in force, where applicable.

What does it pay for?

It pays all sums for which the Insured shall become legally liable to pay as compensation for physical loss or destruction or damage to goods or merchandise, while in transit, including during loading or unloading and while temporarily housed on or off vehicles in the ordinary course of transit under contract or international convention.

Possible policy extensions

Cover can be extended to include legal costs and expenses incurred in litigation against the carrier, removal of debris and cover for sub-contractors.

Delay, loss of market and consequential loss can be covered at additional perils to the policy cover will entail additional premium charges.

General exclusions

The policy will include various exclusions including but not limited to the following:

Carriage of illicit, illegal, contraband or smuggled goods, willful misconduct of the Insured, theft or dishonesty on the part of the Insured's employees, disappearance of or unexplained inventory shortage, defective or inadequate packaging or insulation, deterioration to goods caused by change in temperature resulting from breakdown of any refrigeration equipment and accidents as a result of driver being under influence of alcohol or drugs. Inherent defect or vice, wear and tear, deterioration, spontaneous combustion or decay of perishable goods are also excluded.

Moreover, policies will usually exclude certain type of goods such as jewelry, gold, silver, precious stones, bullion, cash, banknotes, deeds, bonds, bills of exchange and other documents representing money.

The policy may well also exclude a certain amount which the Insured shall bear referred to as the policy excess or the deductible.

Setting the sum insured or the liability limit

The Insured may select the max limit of liability required on any-one-shipment basis or on any-one-carrying-vehicle basis, in accordance with the terms of the contract of carry agreed with the sender or the receiver of goods.

Insurers may additionally apply a limit of liability for each and every loss event or a general aggregate limit during the period of insurance.

Policy premium calculation

Premium rates may vary depending on the limit per any one consignment, the general nature of goods carried and the experience of the carrier.

For the purpose of calculating the annual premium, there are usually two methods:

The first uses the number of vehicles employed by the business as the base for the calculation which is multiplied by an annual premium rate linked to the maximum estimated value of goods carried by each vehicle.

The second method works differently, a premium rate per one hundred dollar is multiplied by the estimated annual carry to arrive at the annual policy premium.

What information do the insurers need to be told in an insurance application?

Insurers writing this coverage will be interested in learning about the business, type of goods handled, radius of transit, number and type of vehicles owned and hired, whether contracts are sub-contracted, state of maintenance of vehicles and security arrangements for goods whilst transported and warehoused.

Estimated annual gross freight earnings as a principal carrier and freight paid to subcontractors will be needed as well as the desired maximum liability for any one vehicle and the Insured's past accidents and claims experience.

SECTION 2

THE CARRIER'S LIABILITY INSURANCE POLICY

A COMMON MISCONCEPTION

The goods are insured by the manufacturer so there is no need to purchase an insurance policy!

In legal jargon, the carrier is considered as a *bailee for reward*, meaning the carrier takes custody of some goods in return for a charge, the Insured i.e. the carrier, would then be responsible for the safety of their customers' (i.e. bailor's) goods and any loss in their custody may result in a claim from the subrogated cargo Insurer or the customer themselves.

Recent research findings and developing trends relating to the goods transportation industry

Trucking is big business. If we take the US economy as an example, we'd find large dependence on truck delivery amounting to ten billion tons of goods that is more than 80% of all freight transported annually in the U.S. which is estimated at USD700.4 billion worth of goods. US trucking business is forecast to grow 21% from 2013 to 2023. Additionally, the Department of Transportation in the US, projects freight tonnage to increase 62% by 2040.

Interesting studies from Europe have shed some light on the nature and size of haulage contractors, according to the Road Haulage Association (UK), 87% of haulage companies have fewer than five vehicles, while over half have just one. The majority of these businesses are family run operating only a few vehicles. Though many goods are hauled for long distances both within the UK and overseas, very many freight journeys are made over relatively short distances, the UK's Department for Transport

(DtF) has found, approximately 52% of goods carried are hauled less than 50 kilometers.

Welcome to the sharing economy. The haulage market is witnessing the emergence of new types of services to challenge traditional ones. Sharing transport offers the ability to leverage spare capacity without making large investments, for example, personal cars, vans and trucks are being used to transport goods and making deliveries. This is an area that has been enabled by the rapid expansion in internet and mobile technologies enabling consumers as well as businesses to arrange delivery at fraction of the cost of the traditional carriers and at faster delivery times through the use of mobile apps installed on their smart devices. This, no doubt is already signaling fundamental changes in the haulage ecosystem.

Case Studies

The following claims scenarios highlight the range of potential accidents that could arise in the normal course of business.

CASE 1: The driver of an express carrier was transporting parcels along the highway in a small van. He drove very fast and caused a rear-end collision with the vehicle in front of him. The parcels were jolted forward sustaining some damage.

CASE 2: Goods were delivered overnight to the carrier's office. During the night, there is a break in and the goods are stolen. The carrier was to blame for not providing round the clock security.

SECTION 2

THE CARRIER'S
LIABILITY INSURANCE
POLICY

CASE 3: The engine compartment of a truck operated by a transportation company carrying various types of electronic goods catches fire which engulfs all the carried cargo. In Dubai, the high summer temperatures exceeding 50 degrees Celsius combined with ill maintained engine contributed to the combustion in the engine compartment.

The Commercial General Liability Insurance Policy

Small businesses, corporations and even not-for-profit organizations may face liability exposures for their activities. Though it may be the last thing on anyone's mind until it happens, at worst it can threaten everything a business worked so hard to achieve.

It is apparent that on a global scale, the number of lawsuits being filed against businesses is both surprising and alarming and even if it is thought that a claim is unlikely to happen, a business can be sued for almost any reason ranging from negligence, personal injury, slander and faulty products to advertising misprints.

The awards for serious injuries can be enormous, for instance if a lawsuit is brought in the USA, awards can be significantly high especially when punitive damages are awarded and can run into millions of dollars not counting the associated legal expenses and defence costs.

Who is the policy suitable for?

SECTION 2

THE COMMERCIAL GENERAL LIABILITY INSURANCE POLICY

It's fair to say that almost every business needs general liability insurance because there is always a risk of injury to anyone just by being on the premises. Some employers might also require the Insured to carry a certain amount of general liability insurance before work is carried-out for them.

Cover description

Insurance cover is generally written on "occurrence basis" and is designed to cover business owners and operators from a wide variety of liability exposures resulting from non-professional negligent acts, most commonly including the following:

- Bodily injury to a third party causing sickness or disease to a person including death
- Property damage to tangible property belonging to a third party including all resulting loss of use of that property
- Personal and Advertising injury
- Personal injury, is injury resulting from for example, libel, slander, defamation, wrongful eviction, false arrest and detention, and
- Advertising injury, is injury resulting from for example, violating a person's right of privacy, infringing copyrights or patents or trademarks.
- Product and completed operations liability
- Product liability, is that resulting from injury or damage to a user from a product supplied by the manufacturer, distributor or retailer, and
- Completed operations, is liability resulting from injury or damage for work done away from Insured's premises and the work causing the injury is completed or abandoned.
- Medical payments for bodily injury caused by an accident

What does it pay for?

The Commercial General Liability policy can cover the costs of accident investigation expenses, legal teams, court and witness fees, court judgments and settlements incurred by the Insured as a result of claims for property damage and bodily injury brought by a third party.

Possible policy extensions

Policy coverage can be extended to include cover for protection against acts of negligence by independent contractors, sudden and accidental pollution, contamination liability and employer's liability.

Adding additional coverage to the policy will entail additional premium charges.

General exclusions

The policy will include various exclusions, some of those most frequently used include professional indemnity claims, employer liabilities, motor vehicle or aircraft or watercraft related liabilities, product recall, punitive damages, intentional acts, aircraft products, liquor liability, pollution and asbestos claims, war and war like operations, workmen compensation and property damage to property owned by or hired to or in the custody or control of the Insured or any employee or any party acting on behalf of the Insured.

Contractual liability is excluded under the basic policies unless such obligations would have existed in the absence of the contract.

Sometimes a certain excess may apply for third party property damage but not for bodily injuries claims.

Setting the liability limit

The Insured should make an assessment of the limits required based on the type of service or products they supply and their potential exposure to loss.

The limit of liability would normally be fixed per any one occurrence and usually there is a ceiling on the number of occurrences payable during the policy period by way of a general annual aggregate.

The per occurrence Limit is the most an insurer will pay for the sum of damages for bodily injury and property damage combined arising out of any one occurrence. Any such sums paid will reduce the amount of the applicable aggregate limit available for any other payment. Though, some policies may be issued without an annual aggregate.

Policy premium calculation

The policy rate is calculated based on the business classification that applies to its operations, the size of its business, its location and obviously its past claims experience.

Depending on the business classification, the rate will be applied to the total annual payroll or the number of employees or the gross annual sales or premises area or units.

If we took the estimated annual turnover of the business as the basis for calculating the premium, the premium rate per one thousand dollar is multiplied by the estimated total turnover to arrive at the annual policy premium.

What information do the insurers need to be told in an insurance application?

Proposal forms are used to collect details of past accidents and claims experience, details of the business operation, number of employees, type of services or products it deals in, forecast volume of sales, territory involved, policy limits of liability and the general professional experience of the business.

The Insured must specify whether a claims-made or a claims-occurred coverage trigger is wanted and the retroactive date of insurance.

A COMMON MISCONCEPTION

Personal liability of business owners would be protected if a limited liability company (LLC) is setup!

A common misconception of a limited liability company or an incorporated company (LLC or Ltd.) is that a business owner can be protected from personal liabilities and that liability insurance would not be necessary.

Regardless of the Insured's corporate structure, companies and their corporate executives can be sued and held personally liable if damage or injury had been inflicted on others as a result of doing business.

Recent research findings and developing trends on liability claims

A study published in 2014 on global liability claims trends, found that personal injury and wrongful death claims resulted in more than 44% of claims paid by insurers while third party property damage claims were only 12% of claims. In contrast, personal injury claims were only 8% of total number of claims made compared to property damage being more than three times as many as bodily injury claims.

Indeed over the past few years insurers in the USA, have been taking various affirmative steps to limit their potential exposure for bodily injury claims on construction site related risks for instance. This directly affects insurance policies covering contractors and insurers have looked to apply restrictive endorsements when a gap in policy wording was found. Amendment is being made to the "employer's liability exclusion" in the commercial general liability policy to exclude cover for bodily injury to employees of "any insured" as opposed to the standard clause which applies to exclude cover for employees of "the insured".

Despite the best efforts of insurers to limit their costs and businesses to introduce better risk management plans, the global trend is that of continued rise in ligation costs and this is in many ways directly linked to inflationary pressures in legal action expenses and medical treatment costs.

What is also alarming is the rise of cross border litigation which presents huge challenges to businesses in having to defend against claims under different laws and different jurisdictions and not only that but action could arise across multi-jurisdictions as a result of a single accident.

Case Studies

The following claims scenarios highlight the range of potential accidents that could arise in the normal course of business.

CASE 1: An Insured, who is a sub-contractor is employed to paint the exterior walls of a 5 storey building on a jobsite, fails to properly secure the area and accidently drops the paintbrush on the head of another sub-contractor employee badly injuring his head.

CASE 2: An elderly visitor walks into the lobby of an insured hotel and slips on the marble floor and breaks his pelvis a minute after it had been mopped up.

CASE 3: An Insured who is a domestic fire detector manufacturer, places an advertisement in the newspaper falsely naming one competitor that they sell unreliable detectors.

SECTION 2

THE COMMERCIAL
GENERAL LIABILITY
INSURANCE POLICY

16

The Contractors/Erection All Risks Insurance Policies

(Builder's Risk / Course of Construction Insurance)

Performing contracting work on a construction project is a complex task. Course of construction accidents, timelines, change orders and contract administration are all concerns.

Any building or development is a big financial undertaking, whether it's home improvement in one's own home, property development in the commercial world or feats of engineering for the public good.

As a building is constructed, the risk of loss changes with every phase, from the hole in the ground right up until the building is completed. The values accumulate rapidly towards the end of the project as the structure nears completion. At any time, a loss to work and material could cause financial harm to not only the project owner and any lenders they've borrowed from, but also

SECTION 2

THE CONTRACTORS/ ERECTION ALL RISKS INSURANCE POLICIES

the general contractor and the subcontractors who have invested time and work into the project.

It would be impossible to enumerate all the risks which may arise during the progress of construction projects but one thing that can be highlighted is the need to protect the capital invested in labor, materials and equipment supplied for construction or renovation or building extension projects.

Who is the policy suitable for?

The Contractors All Risks policy (CAR) is normally purchased by project developers, contractors, sub-contractors, project managers, project consultants and other project participants.

This policy is able to accommodate construction and erection projects of any shape, form or size, for instance, minor house redevelopment, the construction of a villa or even a sky scraper, installation and testing of gas turbines for an electric power station, the installation of a printing press, turnkey biscuit factory construction and many such examples.

This policy is regularly taken out in joint names of the contractor and the employer. Parties involved in the project, such as engineering consultants, financiers and others often ask to be added as a joint name to protect their respective interest and will be treated as though each had a separate policy. The idea is that if damage occurs to the insured property then, regardless of who is at fault, insurance compensation will be available to allow for reinstatement.

Cover description

By definition, the intention of the policy is to cover the widest range of un-named risks except those specifically mentioned in the exclusions section of the policy wording therefore the onus is on the insurer to prove that the loss is not admissible.

The policy will provide insurance against loss or damage to the building structure, materials and supplies, machinery, equipment, fixtures designed to be a permanent part of the fabrication, erection, installation, alteration, completion of a construction project while at the project site, materials in transit or at any temporary location. Additionally cover for third party claims due to personal injury or property damage to passers-by, existing and surrounding communities and businesses, directly resulting from construction activity.

Typically a Contractors or Erection All Risks policy is split into two distinctive sections:

Section one: relates to material damage

The policy will indemnify the Insured for loss or damage to the building or other property whilst under construction or erection or to existing structure in which the construction is being carried out.

Section two: relates to third party liability

The policy will indemnify the Insured against their legal liability towards third parties for bodily injury and property damage resulting from the construction work.

The common causes of loss or damage covered under the policy:

- Fire, lightning and explosion
- Faulty manipulation or handling

- Water damage, flood, storm, typhoon, collapse, landslide, earthquake, volcanic eruption and tsunami (natural hazards may be restricted in certain regions)
- Burglary, theft and malicious damage
- Consequences of defective material and workmanship

Contractors All Risks versus Erection All Risks, what is the difference?

The difference in insurance cover between a Contractors All Risks and an Erection All Risks (EAR) policy is minor. An EAR policy is used for projects involving the erection or installation of plants and equipment rather than civil construction. The notable difference is the possibility of including insurance cover for testing and commissioning, plant is on-load or off-load before delivery to the owners.

North American Policy Characteristics – OCIP and CCIP

The Contractors/Erection All Risks policy referred to above is considered the more conventional type of policy wording used internationally. However, the North American markets have developed several variations on the atypical CAR/EAR wording called, wrap-up programs, most notably the *Owner Controlled Insurance Programs* (OCIP) which is purchased by the project owner and the *Contractor Controlled Insurance Programs* (CCIP) purchased by contractors.

Typically, these policies provide added coverage to the standard builders risk cover and may include additional cover for workers compensation, employers liability, commercial general liability, errors and omission, real property, automotive and equipment.

The construction contract signed between the owner and the main contractor is what determines whether an OCIP or a CCIP policy will be in place.

What does it pay for?

The policy provides under section one of the policy for the cost of reinstatement or repair of permanent and temporary works damaged following an accident.

Under section two, the policy pays for the costs and expenses of defending against legal action brought against the Insured by passers-by, existing or surrounding communities and businesses, payment of compensation and damages awarded by the court.

Possible policy extensions

Most common extensions will include cover for the duration of the maintenance or defects liability period, cover for owned and hired-in plant and machinery, cost of removal of debris, cross liability, express freight and air freight charges, loss of workers tools and personal effects, overtime charges, professionals fees, additional customs duties, escalation costs, damage to owner's existing and surrounding property, delay in start-up, vibration damage, damage while in transit, property in temporary storage, fire department service charge, removal or weakening of support and loss of site plans, blueprints, etc.

Adding additional perils and extending coverage will entail additional premium charges.

General exclusions

A list of standardized policy exclusions is widely used and excludes construction equipment and tools, faulty design and faulty workmanship, wear and tear, loss or damage due to gradual deterioration, rectification of aesthetic defects, atmospheric condition losses, rusting, penalties of any nature, non-fulfillment of terms of contract, inventory losses, willful negligence, cessation of work, defective material, seepage, pollution and contamination, war, nuclear and radioactive contamination and consequential losses.

A deductible for each and every loss may be applicable under some sections of the policy.

Setting the sum insured

The sum insured determined under section-one of the policy should represent the total contract value inclusive of the estimated cost of labor charges and cost of materials but excluding land value. The construction budget is the best source for determining the appropriate sum insured.

For projects running for more than two years, there is bound to be noticeable escalation in prices of materials and labor due to market inflationary pressures. The basic policy will pay claims only as per the original cost and price of project however an *escalation clause* can be opted for to take care of such increase in prices.

A policy endorsed with an *escalation clause* allows the sum insured under the policy to be automatically increased by a certain pre-agreed percentage (ranging from 10 to 20%), despite the premium being based on the original estimated sum insured. Infrequently, insurers may insist on additional premium being charged.

In respect to section-two of the policy relating to third party liability (TPL), a limit per-accident and a limit per-policy period may be set by the insurer. Insurers do not usually allow the TPL limit to exceed 30% of the sum insured set under section one.

Policy premium calculation

The best rates are reserved for contractors that are safety-oriented, closely adhere to regulations and guidelines and take all possible steps to protect their projects from damage. Contractors that have a consistent and successful track record in similar type of projects in and a solid reputation for completing their work on time are always at an advantage.

Projects where there is prolonged exposure to congested residential areas or areas of high traffic or regions exposed to natural catastrophes, such as earthquake areas or flood zones and projects that are complex in nature or design or make use of new construction materials will definitely attract higher rates of premium.

A premium rate per one thousand dollar of the sum insured will be multiplied by the total sum insured determined under section one of the policy to arrive at the policy premium for the duration of the project.

There are no tariffs or fixed premium rates of general application for this policy. This is due to the fact that each construction project must be analyzed according to its specific features and technical considerations, which are invariably different in each case.

What information do the insurers need to be told in an insurance application?

A proposal form is the best way for an insurer to get the detailed information required. Questions will relate to details concerning contractor's past accidents experience and claims, a description of the project, soil test reports, depth of excavation, site or plant layout, a method statement compiled by the architect noting the nature and methodology of the works, time frames for each stage and overall duration of project, information on third party properties adjacent to the worksite, contractor's experience in executing similar projects and the technology used in performing the project whether its proven or prototype.

Given the wide variety of policy extensions, a good proposal form will include a list of the available policy extensions for the Insured to tick through. If this is not the case the Insured would be best advised to attach a list of those desired extensions.

A COMMON MISCONCEPTION

The fire or property all risks insurance policy will automatically provide cover whilst an extension is being built to an existing building!

This is not necessarily the case and should always be referred to the existing building insurer and if this insurer is unable to cover the existing building whilst the extension is under construction, then a contractors all risks policy should be purchased and extended to include existing and surrounding properties to cover the risks during construction to untouched parts of the existing building.

Recent research findings and developing trends on the cost of construction claims

Globally, earthquakes rank as the costliest cause of loss on construction sites constituting 65% of total claims paid. The cost of natural catastrophe claims is likely to rise as economic activity and the value of assets in hazardous zones increases.

Human and operator error is ranked second at 12% closely followed by fires and explosion accidents at 8 and 7 % respectively. Fires and explosions could occur because of myriads of reasons ranging from unfinished piping, leaking gas, flammable liquids, explosives to incomplete electrical systems.

A visible trend among large contractors in the last few decades has been the move away from the performance of physical construction trades. In the past, main contractors employed multi-disciplinary manual workforces. However, nowadays, much of the construction activity risk is assigned to subcontractors which meant reducing the main contractor's ability to control the quality of work or ensuring that work is completed on time and on budget.

Case Studies

The following claims scenarios highlight the range of potential accidents that could arise in the normal course of business.

CASE 1: During the excavation work on a building site, a gas line broke after an excavator dug through the ground and hit it. The police had to close off the area and evacuate the community residents for fear of gas explosion.

CASE 2: A building contractor left his plant, tools and equipment on the construction site overnight. The site was broken into and tools worth thousands of dollars were stolen.

CASE 3: A giant tower crane used during construction work for the expansion of the grand mosque in Mecca crashed into the mosque after being buffeted by strong winds and rain killing and injuring more than 200 people.

SECTION 2

THE CONTRACTORS/
ERECTION ALL RISKS
INSURANCE POLICIES

The crane had detached from its anchoring and smashed through the roof of the mosque destroying part of this mega structure.

The Contractors Plant and Equipment Insurance Policy

For construction contractors, large and small, plant and equipment may form a large part of their invested capital and accidental damage to their equipment could cripple the business for prolonged periods until repaired or replaced.

The risk of theft has become greater as large number of mobile equipment can be started with the use of a single common key. As technology has developed, plant has become more compact and so has the diversity of potential risks.

Frequently in recent times, the construction industry has featured in the headlines for all the wrong reasons specially were accidents are involved. Availability, accessibility and appropriate equipment for the job, good skilled operators and mechanics for operating and maintaining that equipment are key aspects to the business of contractors to ensure timely completion of construction projects.

SECTION 2

THE CONTRACTORS PLANT AND EQUIPMENT INSURANCE POLICY

The exposure to risks on construction sites is varied and significant but the level of skill and experience of the plant and equipment managers and operators are essential resources for managing such risks to contribute to the profitability and growth of the business.

Who is the policy suitable for?

A contractor's plant and equipment policy covers a very wide range of equipment, from stationery equipment such as conveyor systems and concrete batching plants to portable tools and large earthmoving equipment such as bulldozers and loading trucks, mobile and tower cranes, temporary buildings and site installations such as office, accommodation and workshop mobile units, concrete plants and electrical generators.

Cover description

The most common form is an all risks policy, the general intention of which is to cover the widest range of unnamed risks occurring by external force, except those specifically mentioned in the exclusions section of the policy.

The policy covers all locations where the insured equipment is parked at or while under repair or where it performs its activity and during its transit to or from job sites by any means of transport (except if it uses its own power) within an agreed geographical area.

Common accidental loss or damage causes the policy provides cover against:

- Incorrect operation or negligent acts of employees
- Forces of nature, such as storm, flood, hail, inundation, landslide, earthquake and volcanic eruption (restricted in certain regions)

- Fire and lightning
- Burglary and theft
- Collision, overturning, falling or things or rocks falling
- Any other accident not excluded under general and special exclusions

What does it pay for?

The policy provides protection for cost and expenses of recovery, towing and repair of damaged equipment or reimbursement for the cost of a replacement if plant or equipment is written off.

Possible policy extensions

The policy may be extended to include inland transit damage, incidental third party liability, increased cost of working following a loss, lease payments, express freight, overtime charges, air freight, recovery of immobilized plant, the loss of keys and professional fees for claim preparation.

Extending the policy coverage will entail additional premium charges.

General exclusions

Typically, the policy excludes coverage for mechanical and electrical breakdown, wear and tear, corrosion, consequential loss, willful acts by the Insured, war or the like, nuclear contamination and third party liability.

Exclusions will also include specific types of machinery or tools for example, tunneling and underground mining plant, plant working on platforms on the water's edge or on barges or on pontoons, elevator or conveyor belts, ropes, belts, tyres and batteries.

Also, vehicles licensed for general road use (except when being used exclusively on a specified construction location off public roads), waterborne vessels and aircrafts are excluded.

A deductible for each and every loss will apply under the policy.

Setting the sum insured

Generally, the contractors plant and equipment Insurance policy stipulates that the total sum insured should represent the total reinstatement value of all the equipment. Reinstatement cost represents the cost of replacement with a similar piece of equipment in addition to the cost of installation, shipping, taxes and customs.

Policy premium calculation

Premiums can be significantly improved by when job sites are secured against vandalism and theft, immobilizing equipment outside business hours, having a plan to evacuate the equipment in case of fires or natural disasters, securely storing equipment when not at job sites, keeping equipment under scheduled maintenance and equipment operators being of adequate skill and experience.

The loss experience of the contractor should be clear of frequent collisions or overturns if equipment is operated in rough terrain, on steep inclines or near rivers or lakes or sea otherwise premium rates will attract a substantial loading to compensate for this extra risk.

The total replacement value for all the equipment insured forms the base of calculating the premium.

A premium rate per one hundred dollar of the sum insured will be multiplied by the total replacement value to arrive at the annual policy premium.

What information do the insurers need to be told in an insurance application?

The insurers will require an itemised list containing description of each piece of equipment including its specifications and year of make, hired-in and hired-out equipment, the repair facilities and the extent of maintenance or servicing available, availability of replacement parts, territorial location and details concerning past accidents and claims.

Specific questions will focus on the work environments the equipment is deployed in for instance information must be given on mining and underground operations, work at or near water, work in heavy weather or close to flood regions and the procedures in place to evacuate equipment.

A COMMON MISCONCEPTION

The warranty trap!

Manufacturer warranties are a promise to repair or replace a product if it has factory damage or is faulty and to provide routine service such as periodic calibration and cleaning, usually valid for a limited time period, some warranties exclude labor charges and others may require the owner to ship the object to factory for service. The majority however, provide coverage only if product is maintained or used as directed by the manufacturer.

SECTION 2

THE CONTRACTORS PLANT AND EQUIPMENT INSURANCE POLICY

Therefore it's important not to overlook a whole lot of risks that are not covered by warranties. Most importantly, external accidental damage due for instance to operator error and other manmade or natural accidents.

Recent research findings and developing trends on equipment management

It is estimated that major causes of loss to contractor's equipment include fire, theft and vandalism. Natural disasters and weather related perils whilst not the first risks to come to mind but can also have a quick and destructive effect on plant and equipment if contractors ignore climatic forces. Perhaps not so surprisingly, most of the losses are most influenced by lack of training, inattention and carelessness.

Additionally, contractors face pressures emanating from budget problems, time constraints, quality of the project and also improving the safety standards.

Consequently, equipment management is a role that has gained more recognition among contractors and is proving to be a vital one. It is a broad term involving the training of drivers and equipment operators, assessment and procurement of equipment, keeping an equipment register, equipment storage, equipment maintenance, replacing and upgrading of equipment and its disposal.

Case Studies

The following claims scenarios highlight the range of potential accidents that could arise in the normal course of business.

CASE 1: Two 14 year olds break into a marina construction site at night and steal a wheel loader. The joyriders drive off with the loader and suddenly lose traction and smack into parked shipping containers.

CASE 2: A collision occurs on a mining site between an excavator and a jumbo articulated dump truck carrying 30 tons of earth resulting in extensive damage to excavator when the truck accidently reversed into the excavator.

CASE 3: During restoration work to a bridge, two cranes were lifting in tandem a section of the bridge when one of cranes fell into the water dragging the second crane in with it and flattening a row of houses and injuring at least 20 people in the aftermath.

SECTION 2

THE CONTRACTORS
PLANT AND
EQUIPMENT
INSURANCE POLICY

The Cyber Liability Insurance Policy

People have become more reliant on electronic commerce and telecommunication and as businesses collect and maintain ever more granular pieces of information on their customers and their employees, the opportunity for hackers and intruders to exploit security gaps and to benefit from such sensitive data has caused increased difficulties for business and the public.

Contrary to popular belief cyber-attacks aren't only limited to lone teenagers but may come from a variety of other sources including, nation states, terrorists, criminals, activists and company insiders.

Hackers primary intention is to steal money or information that can eventually be monetized, such would include, credit card numbers, health records, personal identification information and tax returns. While hackers may directly steal money from customers, the actual cost to business of the data breach comes from lawsuits, loss of business, fines, or other indirect costs.

SECTION 2

THE CYBER LIABILITY INSURANCE POLICY

Unfortunately, there are no data security products, firewalls, or other software that can completely protect a business or its clients from a data breach. Even a well-crafted data privacy policy disclosing the risks in a website, for example, disclaimers cannot prevent lawsuits being brought against a business.

Managing cyber risks through insurance is a relatively new concept, however it is expected to grow exponentially over time as business gradually become more aware that current business insurance policies do not cover cyber or IT related risks. The most rapid adoption of these policies as a risk transfer option has been in those countries that have mandatory data breach notification laws and where government agencies have been more actively involved in policing the corporate response.

Who is the policy suitable for?

Cyber liability insurance is designed for businesses that engage in various electronic activities, such as selling on the internet or collecting data within its computer network.

Companies that provide software as a service, web hosting services or data storage services and online shops are at the most risk, but any IT dependent provider that handles private client information should also consider purchasing this coverage.

Cover description

Cyber liability insurance provides cover against loss or damage suffered by the business and its liability towards third parties regardless of the cause and whether intentional or not. Some of the best available policies will cover the following on a loss occurring basis (rather than claims-made basis):

1. **Third party liability**
   Cover for claims towards customers, clients and employees resulting from security failure of the Insured's network and failure to protect data (privacy liability) and failure to disclose a security failure or privacy breach.

2. **First party direct costs**
   The costs incurred by the business following a security failure or privacy breach and expenses necessary for mitigating such loss.

3. **Business interruption claims**
   Reimbursement for loss of income and operating expenses resulting from a network security failure

Cyber liability insurance is still a fairly new concept which means there is a lot of variation among policies and a lot of room for negotiation with insurers.

What does it pay for?

The policy pays for costs involved in investigating, rectifying and compensating the aftermath of an occurrence of a cyber-accident and pays for the expenses associated with the defence of lawsuits. Here are some common examples:

- Damages or judgments related to the breach
- Cost of responding to regulatory inquiries
- Regulatory fines and penalties
- Liability to banks for re-issuing credit cards and credit monitoring
- Customers notification expenses
- Computer program and electronic data restoration expenses
- Costs of forensic investigation of the breach
- Legal advice to determine notification and regulatory obligations

- Public relations expenses
- Loss of profits and extra expense during the time that the network is down

Possible policy extensions

Additional coverage may be made available to include any of the following at additional premium charges:

- Cyber extortion threat reimbursement, for extortion expenses resulting directly from a credible threat to the Insured's computer system

- Cyber terrorism reimbursement, for income loss, interruption, and special expenses directly incurred as a result of an interruption or failure of the Insured's computer system caused by an act of terrorism

- Media liability cover for infringement, violation or misappropriation of copyright or trademarks

- Acts and omissions by third parties, for instance when the Insured uses the services of a third party vendor to maintain its customer or employee information in the "cloud" and the vendor experiences a data breach, in this event the Insured could be sued by its customers or employees.

General exclusions

Most notable policy exclusions include loss or damage caused by fire, smoke, explosion, lightning, wind, flood, earthquake, hail, power or utility or satellite or telecommunication failure not under the control of the Insured, acts of terrorism or sabotage, seepage or pollution, wear and tear of computer system or digital assets and also excluding seizure of computer assets or electronic data by act of any government authority.

Many cyber policies exclude cover for data lost from unencrypted devices and certain failures of security software.

Cyber liability policies generally include a monetary excess for each and every loss.

Setting the sum insured and the liability limit

Quantifying potential losses from cyber-attacks is one of the issues businesses struggle with, because damages are more often than not intangible, like the negative impact on the brand name in the aftermath of massive data breach. Business looking for cyber insurance should buy as much cover as they can afford to avoid being vulnerable to excessive losses.

A good starting point is to decide on what types of incidents the Insured would like to have covered and to estimate what costs or expenses cover is wanted for.

This should include Insured's own costs and the costs that others may attempt to claim from the Insured as a result of the incident.

Various indemnity limits will attach to the different covers made available, claims expenses will be included within the available limits and any claim expenses paid will reduce the available limits of insurance and may exhaust them completely.

Policy premium calculation

Policies for cyber liability are more customized than other policies insurers sell and therefore tend to be more costly.

SECTION 2

THE CYBER LIABILITY INSURANCE POLICY

Companies that can demonstrate high quality of people, processes and technology, adhere to industry standards and have cyber risk management strategies and data breach response plans to safeguard its data will receive better insurance premium rates.

Industries such as financial institutions, healthcare and retail that use highly sensitive data are generally considered to be of a higher exposure and subsequently attract relatively higher premiums.

A premium rate per one thousand dollar of the sum insured is multiplied by the estimated annual turnover of the business to arrive at the annual policy premium.

What information do the insurers need to be told in an insurance application?

Insurers writing this coverage will be interested in learning about the type of operation size and scope of the business, the number of customers, the extent of online presence, the type of data collected and stored and the risk management techniques applied by the business to protect its network and its assets.

The insurer will probably want to see the disaster response plan of the business and evaluate it with respect to the business' risk management of its networks, its website, its physical assets and its intellectual property.

Information on how employees and others are able to access data systems, antivirus and anti-malware software, PCI DSS compliance (The Payment Card Industry Data Security Standard), the frequency of updates and the performance of firewalls will be required.

Bearing in mind the rapid progress ensuing in mobile technologies including telematics, it should be expected that more probing enquiries will be made by the insurers to understand the ever expanding electronic mediums used in business.

A COMMON MISCONCEPTION

We are fully protected with the latest firewalls and anti-virus products. Not only that, but some of our data is also hosted in the cloud, so there is no need for cyber liability insurance!

Most people think that data security products will flag security breaches, the reality is that many businesses find out about their security gaps when it is too late and damage has already been suffered. For two-thirds of data breaches, it took months or years for a business to realize its security had been compromised.

Moreover, if the website or any of the data is hosted or stored in the cloud, a good look should be taken at the contract signed with the cloud provider. Customers of cloud providers can't fully control how their data is handled. Therefore, business is still legally responsible for any data breach.

Recent research findings and developing trends relating to cyber incidents

The number of U.S. data breaches in 2015 totaled 781, according to a recent report. The business sector ranked first with nearly 40 percent of the breaches, an increase of 8 percent from 2014 figures. In second place was the health and medical sector with 35.5 percent of the total overall breaches. Accidental email and internet exposure was the third most common source of compromised data

at 13.7 percent. Globally, IBM reported that more than 91 million security events occur per year.

In a different cyber claims study, personally identifiable information was the leader in the type of data exposed. Private health information was a distant second, followed closely by payment card information.

Computers are still the primary target. According to a 2013 study by Verizon of thousands of data breaches, 69% percent of all attacks occur on laptops, desktops, and file servers. While web apps are a substantial source of attacks, most hackers tend to target the more traditional workstations.

An alarming example of a recent type of attack on businesses is a new malware called Ransomware which prevents or limits users access to their data in return for money. Some Ransomware gets the data slowly encrypted until the entire system is totally locked up.

Case Studies

The following claims scenarios highlight the range of potential accidents that could arise in the normal course of business.

CASE 1: During the busiest shopping period of the year, an online retailer of stationary and gifts had its database files infected by malware. Online criminals had encrypted the online database files, making them unusable and were demanding a USD250,000 ransom to unscramble the data. The retailer had to employ the services of an IT security consultant to help in the recovery of their data. The website remained out of business for almost 10 days before it successfully restarted the website.

CASE 2: The website of a maker of headphones that attracts customers from all over the world had to re-setup the website after being hit with a distributed denial of service attack (DDoS) that made the website unavailable. Customers kept emailing the owner to ask if he was still in business. Even though the attack was confined to 8 days, the stress was enormous fearing the complete loss of the database and of having to redesign the entire website.

CASE 3: An employee installed a hacking program on the Insured's company network systems which allowed the employee to override security codes and unencrypt secured passwords gaining full access to the Insured's systems.

The Insured's employee then deleted vital computer files and databases disabling the operation of the company's manufacturing, customer service and administrative systems. The loss was devastating shutting the operation completely for 3 weeks. The business lost 3 years' worth of vital data and returning to full operation needed 2 months. Sizable customers had defected to their competitors.

SECTION 2

THE CYBER LIABILITY
INSURANCE POLICY

The Deterioration of Stock Insurance Policy

Cold room storage is essential for any business involved in manufacturing or distributing food and other perishable products such as fish, meat, fruits, vegetables, ice cream, plants and flowers, helping to keep such products fresh, minimize waste and meet food safety legislation. Proper storage reduces the likelihood of bacterial, microbial and fungal contamination of the stored products, for produce such as fruits and vegetables, time has a direct impact on their shelf life and therefore on the potential revenue to be generated.

Cold room storage is also required for many types of nonedible goods such in the storage of medical products, old photographic films, chemical and other laboratory supplies.

Product expiration dates are based on ideal storage conditions and protecting product quality until their expiration date is important for serving customers and conserving resources.

SECTION 2

THE DETERIORATION OF STOCK INSURANCE POLICY

Whenever there is storage of perishable goods in refrigerated environments there is a risk of loss or damage from fluctuations in temperature due to the breakdown of the cooling equipment. Fluctuations in temperature can include undesirable high or extremely low temperatures leading for instance to rotting, diseases or weight loss due to shrinkage.

For example, fruits, if temperature range is exceeded this can possibly lead to damage such a color change, softening, unwanted or premature ripening, texture degradation and the development of rots and molds, all of which can reduce its value and marketability.

Who is this policy suitable for?

The deterioration of stock policy can be used by the goods owner storing goods in own cold stores or in public cold stores. The policy is also regularly taken out by owners of cold stores lease their space to others.

The owners of cold stores usually work under contract conditions relieving them of all responsibility for damage to goods. However, in the interest of good business, it is usual to find, that liabilities for deterioration of stock resulting from a defect in the cold storage are accepted.

Cold stores can be found in hotels, restaurants, butcher shops, supermarkets, hospitals, food factories, pharmaceutical factories, medical labs, airport kitchens and bonded cold stores.

These stores come in many different shapes and sizes, it could have one single room or it can be divided into a number of rooms. It could also be a single storey or a multi-storey warehouse-style building. Stores can be categorized as production stores, bulk stores, distribution stores or retail stores depending on the business operation involved.

Some of options the owners of goods have in storing their precious products include:

- Walk-in cold stores room
- Free-standing freezer units
- Leased commercial storage space from a reputable company

Cover description

The Policy generally provides cover for accidental loss or damage by rise or fall in temperature leading to deterioration or putrefaction of goods stored in cold stores.

Typically causes of loss or damage covered by the policy include:

- Deterioration due to accidental breakdown of the refrigeration equipment or non-operation of the controlling devices of such equipment
- Accidental failure emanating at the public electricity supply
- Deterioration caused by the action of escaping refrigerant fumes
- Damage to the refrigeration equipment or store structure caused by impact, for example during the operation of a forklift truck

Generally, insurers insist that the cold store is insured against Machinery Breakdown for this policy to be issued.

What does it pay for?

SECTION 2

THE DETERIORATION OF STOCK INSURANCE POLICY

Deterioration of stock insurance will basically replace the goods lost or pay for the lost or damaged goods, reimburse cleaning and decontamination costs and cover the expenses for the disposal of goods.

Possible policy extensions

Generally, policies may be extended to include express freight, holiday and overtime rates of wages and accountants or other professional's fees for claim preparation.

Such extensions to policy coverage will entail additional premium charges.

General exclusions

Common exclusions used in many policies exclude loss or damage resulting from shrinkage, diseases, normal deterioration or natural putrefaction or fermentation, improper storage, stowage or collapse of packing materials, inherent defect, damage to the cold storage chamber, theft, fire, lightning, flood, explosion, aircraft or other aerial devices or articles dropped therefrom, consequential losses, penalties, war or warlike operations, nuclear perils, willful acts, radiation and nuclear energy risks.

A time deductible which could range from a few hours to few days for each and every loss may be applicable under the policy.

Setting the sum insured

Attention must be paid to the way the sum insured is calculated for the stocks held.

In determining the sum insured it is important to estimate the cost price of the stock before deduction of any trade discounts received per each cold store and then multiply by the number of cold stores or chambers. This total value must represent the maximum value of goods held during the busiest periods of business rather than an average of the levels held throughout the year.

Policy premium calculation

Premium rates are influenced by factors such as value of stock in cold storage, age and condition of refrigeration machinery, construction of cold store, nature of goods and the Insured's previous loss history.

The base for calculating the premium is the estimated total value of stocks kept in the cold store and a premium rate per one thousand dollar will be multiplied by the total sum insured to arrive at the annual policy premium.

What information do the insurers need to be told in an insurance application?

Generally the information requirement will include information on the type of goods being stored, estimated value of goods being stored, size and age of the cold store, specifications of refrigeration machinery, the preventive maintenance policy, the general housekeeping and working environment, availability of standby or backup refrigeration and power generation equipment, frequency of temperature checks and the description of temperature control procedures and alarms.

The insurer may additionally want to carry out an inspection of the premises to gather additional information.

SECTION 2

THE DETERIORATION OF STOCK INSURANCE POLICY

A COMMON MISCONCEPTION

This policy is only useful for bonded warehouses and industrial size cold stores!

No, not necessarily. Practically any business that relies on cooling, chilling or freezing of its products will find this policy useful. This includes hotels, restaurants, cafes, hospitals and many others.

The financial loss the business suffers due to lost products will in many instances be mitigated with assistance from an experienced insurer in stemming further losses and assisting the business to return to serving its customers.

Recent research findings and on major problems affecting the cold storage industry

Maintaining the highest product quality possible is top priority for the food processing and pharmaceutical industries requiring housing of these products at precise temperatures.

The most common problems faced by the cold storage industry is the deterioration of the insulation sandwich panels in the walls and roof of the store which can be caused by several factors, for instance, lack of adequate ventilation to reduce humidity, inadequate roof insulation preventing the build-up of water moisture, un-checked roof leaks or overflowing gutters and poor vapor sealing leading to damage of refrigeration pipework.

The effects of such damage could cause varying levels of loss some may be considered minor while others could be potentially catastrophic. Most commonly, damage leads to an increase in energy costs due to loss of thermal insulation or water seepage into the cold store causing ice formation on the products or ceiling panel collapse due to increase in weight or increased loads on the cold store steel structure rendering the store unfit for use.

Case Studies

The following claims scenarios highlight the range of potential accidents that could arise in the normal course of business.

CASE 1: The compressor of a freezer used at a university affiliated medical research laboratory suffered an accidental breakdown which was discovered more than 15 hours after the accident. This has led to the loss of sensitive biological research samples built over many months of work.

CASE 2: A forklift being operated by an employee inside a cold store, collided with the door leading to 500 sq. m cold chamber containing fresh flowers. The collision broke off the door of the chamber and lead the store owner to rent alternative storage space from a competitor to prevent loss of his precious consignment.

CASE 3: The evening cleaner in a five star hotel accidentally disconnected the power supply to an industrial size fridge containing shrimp, fish and other seafood. The accident was discovered the following day. The hotel management insisted that the stock was no longer suitable for human consumption after more than 8 hours without refrigeration.

Useful reading

Storage Guidelines for Fruits & Vegetables. Cornell Cooperative Extension.

Guidelines for the Storage of Essential Medicines and other Health Commodities. DELIVER, World Health Organization (WHO), USAID, UNICEF and JSI, published in 2003.

Directors and Officers Liability Insurance Policy

Company directors and officers have specific responsibilities and powers relating to their positions and the resulting tension between shareholders' expectations of their directors and the ability for a director to meet those expectations is as ever intensifying.

Civil, criminal or regulatory proceedings can be taken if an act of a director or an officer of a company is found to have caused adverse financial consequences to the business. Claims from investors, stockholders, employees, vendors and clients can be made against the company and against its directors who can be held personally responsible for their acts and decisions.

Executive liability has evolved to become a constant threat for corporations large and small for the huge litigation damages, expenses and distractions can inhibit decision making and result in loss of business.

SECTION 2

DIRECTORS AND OFFICERS LIABILITY INSURANCE POLICY

Who is the policy suitable for?

All current, future and past directors and officers of a company and its subsidiaries could be covered under the policy, which can also include non-executive directors.

When a board of directors is assembled, directors will usually make this a requirement. Also, investors and venture capitalists will also require such insurance as part of the conditions of funding the company.

If an IPO is planned, a D&O policy will be crucial because claims can arise if stock performance is not as investors had been led to expect.

Cover description

The policy covers claims resulting from managerial wrongful acts that had adverse financial consequences. Most usually policy is written on claims-made basis.

Wrongful acts may include, for example, breach of trust, breach of duty, neglect, error, misleading statements, misuse of company funds, lack of corporate governance and wrongful trading.

D&O policies are typically structured in the following manner:

1. Directors or officers direct losses that are not indemnified by the company

2. Reimbursement to the company for losses relating to claims made against the directors and officers that the company has indemnified them for

3. Entity coverage (company cover) for claims against the company itself. Though generally limited to losses related to securities claims

4. Cover for losses arising from responding to a stockholder derivative demand

What does it pay for?

A Directors and Officers policy will provide protection to managers against the costs associated with the defence, investigation, negotiation and court settlement of an admissible claim. This will include lawyer fees, court costs, expert or other specialist fees and filing fees.

In addition to expenses, court judgments or verdicts and settlements are also covered.

Possible policy extensions

The policy can be extended to include bodily injury, property damage, dishonest acts, breach of contract, pollution, fines, penalties, employment practices claims and punitive damages for securities claims.

It can be also extended to cover the company itself (as an entity) if it's named in a suit, managers and non-executive directors.

Adding additional perils to the policy cover will entail additional premium charges.

General exclusions

The policy will include various exclusions including but not limited to the risk of fraud, personal profiting, accounting of profits, Insured versus Insured claims, bodily injury, property damage, pollution, war, fines, penalties, hostile takeover or captive insurance company exclusions.

The policy will exclude a certain amount which the Insured shall bear referred to as the policy excess or the deductible.

Setting the liability limit

In fixing the indemnity limit, the Insured must seriously consider the universal trends relating to aggressive plaintiff litigation, increased loss severity and significant regulation scrutiny.

The amount of cover purchased must be enough to cover the awards and the defence costs of all claims.

A company that is actively pursuing mergers and acquisitions, preparing for an initial public offering or has other strategic plans that could increase the risk of claims should take these plans into account when evaluating the adequacy of limits.

The limit of indemnity is shared among all Insureds. For example, one insured's defence fees will reduce the amount of cover available to other Insureds. Because many Insureds usually share in a single pool of insurance cover, this issue needs to be considered carefully when setting the aggregate limit.

Policy premium calculation

Several factors have far-reaching impact on the premiums quoted by insurers, these include internal corporate governance, mergers and acquisitions or going public (IPOs') activities, the financial stability of the business and the industry the business operates in. Businesses in investment, securities and banking, bio-tech and pharmaceuticals are considered riskier than most other sectors.

The Insured will also have to declare if there are any planned redundancies and any turnover from the US or assets there as this will have a bearing on the premium as well.

What information do the insurers need to be told in an insurance application?

A fully completed insurance proposal form is usually mandatory for this type of policy.

The proposal form is designed to glean as much information as possible on circumstances and activities the business is or may become involved in such as mergers, acquisitions, capital raising, corporate restructuring, lay-offs or reductions in workforce, sale and disposal of any company or subsidiary.

These forms are usually very extensive in terms of information collection and questions will be asked about the ownership, shareholders, the directors and the executive team, outside directorship, domicile and international activity especially US exposure, industry sector, stock exchange listing, market capitalization, claims record and professional CVs of management team.

Additionally, the latest annual reports and audited accounts, the last two Interim Statements (where applicable) and any public offer document and listing particulars published in the last 12 months will need to be submitted with the proposal.

SECTION 2

DIRECTORS AND
OFFICERS LIABILITY
INSURANCE POLICY

A COMMON MISCONCEPTION

D&O insurance is only for publicly traded companies!

That's not the case. A business doesn't have to have shareholders in order for its directors and officers to be personally sued. If the business anticipates merger and acquisition activity or deals with customers, vendors, venture capitalists or financiers and others, then there is exposure to such risks.

Moreover businesses of any size will have officers and possibly directors opening the door for legal action against them over the running of their companies.

Recent research findings and developing trends relating to risks faced by company directors!

Following the global financial crisis during 2007-2008 regulators around the world have sought to apply broader regulations and find new ways to make directors and officers responsible for the actions of their companies with particular focus on individuals within large corporations. Indeed a UK business report released in 2014 found that the issue of regulatory and other investigations was perceived by directors as the top risk of concern to them while the risks of "criminal and regulatory fines" and "penalties and anti-corruption legislation" were ranked in second and third place respectively.

What's also surprising was that, just 37% of directors were aware of the proposed expansion by the rule makers and enforcement agencies of the directors' disqualification regime, while non-executive directors were more aware than executive directors, roughly with half of them abreast of these proposals. Non-executive directors tend to have a wider portfolio of directorships, including smaller companies which may be more at risk.

There is also worrying increase in cross-border legal actions, with foreign criminal prosecutions against directors of global companies gaining leverage when it comes to bringing civil claims.

In contrast, in Asia there is much lower preference to litigate than in western cultures. It therefore follows that the risks of being a director in Asia are also far less than in western counterparts. Although, this will change as cross border relationships develop further. What has been recently notable though is the increasing frequency in class action suits against Asian companies on accounting irregularities, which have been targeted by US plaintiff groups.

Case Studies

The following claims scenarios highlight the range of potential accidents that could arise in the normal course of business.

CASE 1: An employee is killed in a fatal accident during his work at a battery manufacturing company. The heirs to the employee's estate and the Health and Safety Executive bring legal action against the directors and the company for compensation.

CASE 2: A bank alleges fraudulent misrepresentation by a company director in a loan application and sues him for repayment and compensation when the business is unable to repay the money lent to it.

SECTION 2

DIRECTORS AND
OFFICERS LIABILITY
INSURANCE POLICY

CASE 3: The administrators of a company in liquidation brought legal action against the Insured's former directors and senior officers alleging they devised a strategy to overstate stockholders equity therefore disguising the Insured's dire financial position.

21

The Electronic Equipment Insurance Policy

Businesses today are completely dependent on electronic data and equipment like laptops, desktops, servers and smart devices. Any loss or damage to such equipment will severely impact the day to day operation of business.

Media headlines about IT failures certainly don't help and while it's perceived by many that idled staff and reduced productivity are the most substantial costs of a downtime, the value of lost opportunities and customer defections are often missed out, in many cases these turn out to be harder to recapture or reverse resulting in bigger financial losses.

For the past two decades, the trend in business has been to reduce operating costs by eliminating labor and then to replace this labor with business process automation that is capable of functioning without human intervention. Systems like these have improved business efficiency and delivered cost savings, but there can also be a dark side.

SECTION 2

THE ELECTRONIC
EQUIPMENT
INSURANCE POLICY

Unfortunately, the myth that many businesses fall into is that maintenance contracts are an alternative to insurance viewing these contracts as a hedge against failures. But the truth of the matter is that equipment will fail at the same rate regardless of the price paid for these contracts.

A lot of times, businesses just don't fully understand the cost of not preparing for accidents and are not willing to spend money to ensure a disaster doesn't occur or that they can recover quickly from a disaster.

Who is the policy suitable for?

The policy can be taken out by a variety of parties such as the owners of the equipment, lessor or lessee, bankers or financiers.

The most important range of equipment to be covered by this policy relates to computers and high value electronic equipment although the variety of equipment that may be considered is endless and may include any electronic device. For example, desktops and laptops, computer servers, radio and TV broadcasting studio equipment, telephone exchanges, satellite telecommunication and mobile transmission trucks, hospital MRI scanners, point of sale terminals, airport security screening equipment, heavy duty office imaging equipment, online broker trading servers and warehouse automation equipment.

Cover description

This policy covers sudden and accidental electrical and mechanical breakdown by any cause or peril not specifically excluded under the policy.

Policy cover is divided in to three sections:

1. **Section one**: provides cover against accidental material damage to equipment

2. **Section two**: provides cover against accidental loss of data media and data stored thereon as result of an accident under Section One

3. **Section three**: provides cover against increased cost of working resulting from accidental loss and or damage to the electronic equipment covered under section one

Example accidents covered under the policy include fire, soot, smoke, smoldering, flood or water damage, burglary, theft, short circuit, excess voltage or induction, faulty operation, lack of skill, negligence, faulty design or defects in material, faults at workshop and faults in erection.

What does it pay for?

Electronic equipment insurance pays for the costs and associated expenses following loss or damage to equipment. More properly protection may include:

1. **Section one**: payment for costs required to repair damage or replace damaged equipment

2. **Section two**: payment for costs and expenses for restoration or recopying of data if backup system is available and the costs of data media replacement

3. **Section three**: payment for all additional costs needed to ensure operational continuity using substitute equipment if such costs arise following loss or damage to equipment insured under the section one

Possible policy extensions

Policies generally may be extended to include express freight, holiday and overtime rates of wages, strikes, riots, civil commotion and accountant's fees for claim preparation.

Such extensions to policy coverage will entail additional premium charges.

General exclusions

A list of standardized policy exclusions is widely used and excludes, willful acts or negligence, wear and tear, aesthetic defects, manufacturer or supplier contractual obligation, incorrect data processing, fraud, loss of data due to a cyber-attack, consequential losses, war or warlike operations, nuclear perils, radiation and nuclear energy risks and theft.

A deductible for each and every loss covered under the policy may be applicable under the various sections of the policy.

Setting the sum insured

The different sections of the policy must be taken into consideration when setting the sums insured, noting the following:

1. **Section one**: naturally the sum insured should be equal to the cost of replacement of the equipment with new one of the same specification, this would represent the present day purchase value of a similar new equipment including all incidental expenses like consultation fees, erection costs, custom duties, freight and insurance and handling charges.

2. **Section two**: the sum insured should be the amount required to restore the insured external data media by replacing lost or damaged data media with new material and reproducing the lost information.

3. **Section three**: the sum insured should represent the hire charges for substitute equipment to ensure continued data processing for the specified indemnity period, including personnel and transportation charges.

Policy premium calculation

The cost of purchasing this insurance depends on the type, make, model, age and nature of equipment being used complemented with the Insured's loss history. Having in place good risk management practices will help in reducing the premium rates offered by insurers.

A premium rate per one thousand dollar will be multiplied by the total sum insured for all equipment insured to arrive at the annual policy premium.

What information do the insurers need to be told in an insurance application?

Generally speaking the information requirement will include details of equipment manufacturers, description of the machinery including specifications, year of manufacture, the extent of obsolescence of the equipment, preventive maintenance arrangements, the general housekeeping and security in the business premises, availability of replacement parts, data backup arrangements, disaster recovery planning and details concerning past accidents and claims.

SECTION 2

THE ELECTRONIC
EQUIPMENT
INSURANCE POLICY

If loss of data and increased cost of working are required the Insured should expect to prepare calculations for sums to be insured and the indemnity period required.

A COMMON MISCONCEPTION

Increased Cost of Working is the same as Business Interruption!

Many businesses fail to understand the *increased cost of working* section of the policy by wrongly believing that it includes compensation for the consequential loss following breakdown or an external accident.

The policy does not cover loss or reduction in revenue or loss of customer resulting from loss or damage to the equipment.

The increased cost of working section relates to the costs of reimbursement of additional expenses involved for hire charges or transportation costs and other similar costs enabling the continuation of business.

Recent research findings and developing trends on major problems affecting electronic equipment failure

In a survey involving 200 companies across North America and Europe it was estimated that on average, businesses suffered 14 hours of IT related downtime per year. Half of those surveyed indicated that their reputation was damaged while 18% categorized the impact as very damaging on their reputation. Most interesting however, almost 90% of respondents pointed out that failure to recover data would be damaging to the business and 23% described that it would be disastrous.

Many experienced maintenance managers would advise the only policy that should be adopted in a business is to buy equipment that does not fail. The cost of maintaining equipment is wasted money and it has become a business norm when buying equipment to expect designs and parts that fail and require maintenance.

Thermal overstress or excess heat is the most common cause leading to semiconductor failure. Excess heat melts materials, warps and breaks semiconductor dies and causes other types of damage.

The sun's burst of solar activity is another cause that could have devastating effects. Analysis of solar storm records from the past 50 years, it was concluded that there is a 12 percent chance of a major solar storm hitting Earth in the next 10 years. It would potentially interfere with radio, GPS and satellite communications, affecting the use of millions of electronics around the world. Power grids would also be affected due to power surges causing major worldwide blackouts similar to the one that occurred in Quebec in 1989. The economic costs are estimated to be in excess of USD1 trillion in the first year of impact, with a full recovery taking more than 4 years according to the National Research Council of Canada.

Case Studies

The following claims scenarios highlight the range of potential accidents that could arise in the normal course of business.

SECTION 2

THE ELECTRONIC
EQUIPMENT
INSURANCE POLICY

CASE 1: A power surge damaged a mega multi-speaker intercom system and an internal clock system of office tower. Many of the intercom's control stations and the clock's electrical components had replacement.

CASE 2: Wrong input voltage causes massive overheating of the electronic chip in a state of the art server and melts the integrated circuit board.

CASE 3: An MRI machine's cooling system for the superconducting magnets lost pressure due to sudden power surge, so the machine had to be taken off service.

22

The Employers Liability Insurance Policy

The rising tide of no-win-no-fee lawyers has meant that many workers now have access to the justice system placing businesses at significant risk, the number of cases brought against employers has continued to increase. A single claim can easily bankrupt a business.

Employers' may find themselves liable not only towards existing employees but also towards former employees many years into the future. Many occupational illnesses take a long time to manifest and as a result businesses may be facing a claim from a past employee several years down the line.

Contractually, all employers have a common-law duty of care towards their employees, to provide a safe place and systems of work, adequate training and supervision. Moreover, they need to make sure they are aware

SECTION 2

THE EMPLOYERS LIABILITY INSURANCE POLICY

of the regulations for their industry and need to carry out regular risk assessments to protect their employees.

In many instances, it has been shown that it is insufficient for employers to attempt to control such risks by way of an employment contract or other workplace agreement as the increasing diversity of recent cases involving disputes with employees have demonstrated time and over again.

Moreover, employees are increasingly suing multiple companies on grounds of joint employer liability. This is typically the case with employees associated with franchisees, subcontractors and staffing agencies or manpower companies.

Who is the policy suitable for?

Unless the business is literally a one-man operation, Employers Liability insurance is something that nearly every business owner needs. Staff that are employed under a contract of service or apprenticeship or are sub-contracted or employed in other capacity satisfying any of the 3 criterions mentioned below should be insured.

Employers Liability insurance is most likely needed if (insurance criterions):

- Insured maintains control of where and how their employees perform their work or
- Workers work under similar conditions and treatment to another member of staff who is covered by the insurance or
- The equipment, materials or premises are owned by the Insured

If the Insured has full time employees, contractors, casual workers, seasonal workers or temporary staff, students and people on work placements, volunteers, advisers, referees and marshals, it is advisable to take out

Employers Liability cover. In some countries, Employers Liability Insurance is required by law, which ensures that the employer has in place the minimum level of cover against such claims (for example, in the U.S. it is combined with the Workers Compensation cover in one policy and businesses in the UK are compelled to hold this type of insurance according to the Employers Liability Compulsory Insurance (ELCI), Act 1969).

Cover description

The intention of the policy is to cover all legal liability claims made against the Insured, whether it is caused on or off the job site or be it the office premises, relating to injury or illness or death of an employee as a direct result of their work while in the employment of the Insured, other than liability imposed on the Insured by a workers compensation law, if applicable.

Employers' liability insurance can be packaged with workers compensation insurance (and referred to as part 2 under such policies) to further protect businesses against the costs associated with workplace injuries, illnesses and deaths that aren't covered under workers compensation.

What does it pay for?

Employers Liability insurance will provide protection against the cost of compensation awarded to employees for injury or illness as well as associated legal defense costs and expenses.

Possible policy extensions

Some of the most common extensions include coverage for injury or illness resulting from terrorism, offshore work or at sea, work overseas, indemnity to directors or employees, court attendance costs and liability resulting from private work carried out by employees of the Insured for any director or executive of the Insured.

Adding additional perils to the policy cover will entail additional premium charges.

General exclusions

Most common policy exclusions include (but are not limited to) bodily injury to any employee carried in or on a vehicle whilst being used on a road, terrorism, asbestos, work on offshore installation (oil rigs for example), liability assumed under a contract, bodily injury intentionally caused or aggravated by the employer, damages arising out of wrongful termination, discrimination, harassment and other workplace related torts and fines or penalties imposed for violation of laws or regulations.

Staff that would not be covered under the policy will include business owners, close family members, an employee while employed in violation of the law with the employer's knowledge, unpaid workers and independent contractors or non-exclusive workers.

Setting the liability limit

If the jurisdiction where the Insured operates makes an employer's liability policy compulsory there would naturally be a legal minimum requirement for the limit of indemnity, though larger businesses may require higher limits exceeding the minimum regulatory requirement depending on the nature of the business and the number of employees.

The limit of liability is fixed per any one occurrence and usually there is a ceiling on the number of occurrences payable during the policy period by way of a general annual aggregate.

Policy premium calculation

The premium quoted by the insurers will be affected by factors such as the claims history, the size of the perceived risk and the approach the business employs towards risk management.

Therefore, the safer the working environment and the fewer claims are made, the lower the risk will be. Premium rates are governed by a tariff related to the nature of business carried on by the Insured.

For smaller businesses the insurers calculate the premium based on the number of employees, this is called a "per capita" rating.

For larger businesses the premiums are rated on the estimated salary roll. A premium rate per one thousand dollar will be multiplied by the total annual salaries to arrive at the estimated annual policy premium.

What information do the insurers need to be told in an insurance application?

The information required by underwriters is very simple and should be readily available to the Insured. Questions will relate to the type of trade or industry of the business, the size of payroll, the number of employees and description of their work, claims history and health and safety record.

There will be additional questions to determine if hazardous materials or dangerous machinery and processes are used in the normal course of business.

SECTION 2

THE EMPLOYERS LIABILITY INSURANCE POLICY

A COMMON MISCONCEPTION

A public liability policy provides cover against this risk!

Public Liability insurance is different. It covers the claims made against the business by members of the public or other businesses, but not for claims by its employees.

Generally speaking, Employers' Liability insurance is compulsory in many countries while public liability insurance is usually voluntary.

Recent research findings and developing trends on work related injuries

Businesses cite the challenges posed by long-tail risks which tend to take many years to manifest as their biggest concern, these include claims for occupational diseases such as asbestosis, industrial deafness and vibration white fingers (VWF).

A report published in the United States of the top 10 riskiest jobs in the U.S. based on the rate of fatal work injuries, were determined to be as follows:

1. Fishermen and related fishing workers

2. Logging workers

3. Aircraft pilots and flight engineers

4. Farmers and ranchers

5. Mining machine operators

6. Roofers

7. Reuse and recyclable material collectors

8. Drivers, sales workers and truck drivers

9. Industrial machinery installation, repair and maintenance workers

10. Police and patrol officers

Estimates produced in 2015 in the UK, show that annually more than 600,000 workers are injured in workplace accidents and a further 500,000 workers suffer a new case of ill health which they believe is caused or made worse by their work.

The burden that litigation places on business directly impacts its ability to produce new goods and services and overall employment. A survey of 500 U.S. CEOs' found that lawsuits caused 36% of their companies to discontinue products, 15% to lay off workers and 8% to close plants.

Case Studies

The following claims scenarios highlight the range of potential accidents that could arise in the normal course of business.

CASE 1: An employee working at a warehouse had his foot severely crushed when the driver of a forklift truck inadvertently drove in to him. The employer it seems had also failed to provide all his staff with safety boots.

CASE 2: A part-time worker at a fast food restaurant had his arm caught in a rotary burger grilling machine resulting in fractures to the wrest and severing of a finger. The employer was well aware that his staff were exposed to this hazard but failed to improve work safety.

CASE 3: A factory worker in the aerospace industry, worked for up to six hours a day soldering metal parts using rosin based soldering wire which produced harmful fumes that are known to cause occupational asthma. She was never given any training or warning about the dangers and was soldering in an enclosed space with inadequate air extraction. Within a few weeks of starting work, she began to suffer from difficulty in breathing and was diagnosed with occupational asthma.

23

The Environmental Liability Insurance Policy

(Environmental Impairment liability insurance)

Industrial development while important for the economic growth and development of society have also proven to be harmful to the environment, effects such as the climate change, pollution to air, water and soil, health issues and extinction of species regularly make media headlines. Environmental pollution risks are complex and new hazards can emerge unexpectedly.

Businesses that use or store substantial quantities of chemicals or hazardous materials that could damage the environment or affect other third party property, run the risk of causing a pollution incident and incurring associated liabilities. Pollution and contamination incidents pose significant risk to public health and safety and the environment.

Expensive claims can be filed by governments and local authorities, other businesses, landlords and people who

SECTION 2

THE ENVIRONMENTAL LIABILITY INSURANCE POLICY

live near the business which can result in serious financial strain to business owners and may force a company into bankruptcy.

The variety of potential environmental hazards is enormous and below are some examples:

- Asbestos and harmful dust products released into the air
- Hazardous materials used in industry and agriculture
- Pesticides and pest control products causing the poisoning of living things and environmental pollution
- Wastewater released by factories, treatment plants and sewers
- Land Pollution caused by leakage from fuel and energy
- Marine and coastal pollution due to discharge of sewage and dumping of waste into the sea
- Air emissions including pollutants emitted by factories resulting in the emission of organic solvents, particles entering the respiratory tract, Sulphur dioxide and nitrogen oxides
- Radiation exposure to both ionizing radiation such as that emitted by radioactive materials, x-ray machines and accelerators and non-ionizing radiation for example emitted by electrical installations, mobile broadcasting centers and lasers.
- Solid waste produced in industrial waste, dry waste, and organic waste
- Noise pollution damaging someone's physical and mental health due to frequent or prolonged exposure to loud noise

Who is the policy suitable for?

It is an insurance policy created specifically for businesses that engage in jobs or production that may have harmful or toxic by-products.

This includes businesses that use environmentally unsafe chemicals or similarly emit harmful products, for example, hair salons, dry cleaning services, garages, junkyards, industrial manufacturers, contractors and factories.

Even those in the services sector need such policy including for example educational and medical establishments, engineering consultants and engineers.

Cover description

Environmental liability insurance is a specialist form of insurance providing cover against financial loss incurred as a result of bodily injury or property damage to third parties and any regulatory action arising from pollution or contamination.

More often than not the policy is written on claims-made basis though increasing number of insurers are providing cover on claims-occurrence basis.

It is important to note insurers especially in the U.S. are increasingly widening the definitions of pollution and pollutants to include legionella, bacteria, low-level radioactive waste, electromagnetic fields and medical infectious pathological wastes.

What does it pay for?

The great majority of policies provide for compensation to third parties, court awarded damages, legal defence expenses, the Insured's own site clean-up costs and the costs of rectification imposed by regulatory authorities.

SECTION 2

THE ENVIRONMENTAL LIABILITY INSURANCE POLICY

Possible policy extensions

Insurers may be willing to extend policy cover to include both offsite and onsite pollution liability, emergency expenses in response to an imminent or substantial threat, crisis management expenses to assist with the expenses associated with public relations and media management, mediation credit for claims disputes, insurance for underground storage tanks, loss of profit, loss of rental income, demolition and removal of debris and errors and omissions.

Extending the policy cover will entail additional premium charges.

General exclusions

The most common exclusions used in environmental liability policies include but are not limited to the following:

- Damage resulting from willful non-compliance with the law
- Bodily injury to any employee of the Insured
- Damage that was intended or should have been reasonably expected by the Insured
- Damage to the Insured's own property, whether rented or owned

Setting the liability limit

The Insured should make an assessment of the limits required based on the type of products they supply or operations they perform and their potential exposure to loss.

The limit of liability is fixed per any one occurrence and usually there is a ceiling on the number of occurrences payable during the policy period by way of a general annual aggregate.

The per occurrence Limit is the most an insurer will pay for the sum of damages for bodily injury and property damage arising out of any one occurrence. Any such sums paid will reduce the amount of the applicable aggregate limit available for any other payment.

Policy premium calculation

Premium reduction offers can be made to businesses that have taken actions to reduce their risks by putting together safety measures, protection systems and a well thought out environmental risk management strategy.

The annual turnover of will be used as the basis for calculating the premium. A premium rate per one thousand dollar of the sum insured will be multiplied by the estimated total turnover to arrive at the annual policy premium.

What information do the insurers need to be told in an insurance application?

The information requirement is normally driven by the type of operation the Insured is engaged in and the purpose of the coverage. This will include information on nature of the operations and substances used or produced or transported, information on on-site underground storage tanks, proximity to residential areas or nature reserves, control measures and safety programs utilized to reduce losses, environmental management plans, latest environmental audits and the past claims history of the Insured.

SECTION 2

THE ENVIRONMENTAL LIABILITY INSURANCE POLICY

A COMMON MISCONCEPTION

Isn't this type of cover available in other types of policies?

No. Traditional insurance products such as Property All Risks, Fire, Public Liability and Contractors All Risks policies provide limited, if any cover for pollution. At best, Public Liability policies may offer cover for third party claims (although not necessarily statutory clean-up costs) arising from sudden and accidental pollution events. Property insurance may provide limited clean-up cover, but only if losses occur as a result of an insured peril.

Such policies are clearly inappropriate for the majority of environmental risks, particularly those associated with historic contamination which is often the key concern.

Recent research findings and developing trends on the major sources of environmental pollution

While oil field drilling and mines are considered among the most risky businesses, many of the largest polluters come from the chemical, pesticide, oil refining, petrochemical, metal smelting, iron and steel, and food processing industries.

Other industries have less potential impact but are still considered highly problematic when it comes to pollution include the textile, leather tanning, paint, plastics, pharmaceutical, paper and pulp industries.

In the United States, as is the case in most industrialized nations, the greatest source of pollution emanated from the industrial community. According to the 2000 Toxics Release Inventory (TRI) of the U.S. Environmental Protection Agency (EPA), roughly 3 million metric tons of toxic chemicals from about 2,000 industrial facilities are annually released into the environment, including nearly 46,000 metric tons of recognized carcinogens.

Major oil spills frequently make the media headlines making the public assume that such spills are common. However, the total volume of oil spillage from ships in this decade has been found to be only one sixth of that spilled in the same period of the last decade. Ironically, what has been going up rapidly is the number of claims filed for compensation as a result of spills.

Where air pollution is concerned, recent research indicates that ozone, at levels below current air quality standards has significant negative impact on worker productivity. A 10 parts per billion (ppb) reduction in the ozone standard would translate into an annual cost savings of approximately USD 1.1 billion in labor expenditure if applied to the whole of the U.S. economy. Roughly 11.8 per cent of the U.S. labor force works in an industry with regular exposure to outdoor environment and this figure would be much higher for middle and lower income countries (Graff Zivin and Neidell, 2010).

In new estimates released in the WHO report, in 2012 around 7 million people died as a result of air pollution exposure. This finding more than doubles previous estimates and confirms that air pollution is now the world's largest single environmental health risk. The new data reveals a stronger link between both indoor and outdoor air pollution exposure and cardiovascular diseases, such as strokes and ischaemic heart disease, as well as between air pollution and cancer.

Noise pollution on the other hand, has emerged as a leading environmental nuisance in the European Region and the public complaints about excessive noise have increased more than ever before.

Case Studies

The following claims scenarios highlight the range of potential accidents that could arise in the normal course of business.

CASE 1: A hardware supply chain was fined by the regulator because several of its home renovation contractors reportedly violated lead paint safety quality standards. The contractors didn't properly establish clean-up or decontamination areas. Claims were filed for bodily injuries.

CASE 2: A hospital's heating equipment and oil tank were apparently working perfectly. Suddenly, heating stops and the heating oil tank is found empty. It later transpires that the tank had developed a leak and 11,000 liters of heating oil escaped into the ground. The leak would have been gradual, perhaps over a 10 or 14 days period resulting in the pollution of a nearby stream and forest.

CASE 3: A restaurant owner had been sued by people residing in the surrounding area due to playing loud music literally all nights of the week and also hosting live bands. The suit alleged that the loud music caused physical discomfort, annoyance, mental distress, pain and suffering and lowered property values.

Useful reading

2014 Environmental Performance Index (EPI). Yale Center for Environmental Law & Policy (YCELP),

Yale University. Center for International Earth Science Information Network (CIESIN), Columbia University. In collaboration with World Economic Forum, Geneva, Switzerland and the support of The Samuel Family Foundation, Toronto, Canada.

SECTION 2

THE
ENVIRONMENTAL
LIABILITY INSURANCE
POLICY

The Fidelity Guarantee Insurance Policy

Businesses run significant financial risks as a result of exposure to crime committed by employees and surveys show that fraud is on the increase corresponding with the growth in the use of electronic data and asset transfers.

Theft takes on almost infinite number of forms, most notable examples include employees stealing cash or merchandise, removing equipment from the office, giving employee discounts to family members or friends, overcharging customers and pocketing the extra money, falsifying records by the use of non-existent employees and receiving kickbacks from suppliers.

Small businesses in particular are most vulnerable because they have fewer employees and these employees may have a wide range of responsibilities within the business along with which comes knowledge of oversight mechanisms.

SECTION 2

THE FIDELITY
GUARANTEE
INSURANCE POLICY

It has been established that employees rarely steal from their employer because of need but thefts usually occur because the chances of getting caught are low.

Who is the policy suitable for?

The fidelity guarantee policy is most often sought by businesses where employees are more likely to cause a financial loss because of their constant exposure to cash, goods and other assets.

Employees occupying positions of trust, such as, cashiers, accountants, salesmen, storekeepers and others handling assets of the business can be covered against stealing money or goods from the business.

Cover description

This Policy broadly covers pecuniary loss sustained as a result of acts of theft (larceny, embezzlement and skimming), fraud or dishonesty against the employer committed by the employee in the course of their duties within a predefined period of discovery, most commonly 12 months beyond the expiry date of policy.

The different assets that employees could steal from their employer are varied and could include money, bullion, travelers cheques, negotiable instruments, bearer bonds or coupons, stamps, cheques, company property, supplies, merchandise, information, trade secrets and even time (by falsifying timekeeping records).

What does it pay for?

The Policy pays the actual financial loss sustained as a result of the dishonesty or fraudulent act of the employee up to the sum insured specified in the policy schedule. The mount payable under the policy is subject to adjustments against any salary, commission, bonuses, end of service indemnity or any other money standing to the credit of the fraudulent employee.

Possible policy extensions

This standard cover of this policy available is regularly extended to include cover for costs of auditors' and accountants' fees incurred in preparing a claim, continuation of insurance coverage if the Insured is subject to a merger or takeover or sale or if wound-up, reinstatement of limit of liability if depleted by claims and the policy may be modified to be issued on un-named employee basis.

Such extensions to policy coverage will entail additional premium charges.

General exclusions

This policy commonly excludes loss resulting from any change in the circumstances or conditions of the employment without the consent of the insurer, loss due to non-observance or relaxation of system of checks and precautions, loss discovered more than 12 months after the termination either of the policy or of the service of employee concerned, consequential losses of any nature and legal liability of any kind.

The policy will exclude a certain amount which the Insured shall bear for each and every claim referred to as the policy excess or the deductible.

Setting the sum insured

The sum insured can be specified individually for each employee or per occupation (for example cashiers,

SECTION 2

THE FIDELITY
GUARANTEE
INSURANCE POLICY

warehouse keepers, finance manager, salesman etc.) and should represent the maximum level of loss that the business could sustain as a result of a dishonest action of one employee acting alone, or several employees acting in collusion, or even employees acting in collusion with third parties.

There may well be an annual limit stipulated in addition to the individually specified limits.

Policy premium calculation

The premium rate is largely determined by the nature of the assets at risk, their liquidity and value, the number of employees and their individual job classification by occupation.

Insurers may allow some premium discount if there is evidence of good security and control in place, there is frequent comprehensive audits and other risk management practices in place.

A premium rate per one thousand dollar would be multiplied by the total sum insured, being the sum of the individually set limits for all of the employees or occupation categories.

What information do the insurers need to be told in an insurance application?

Most proposal forms come in two sections, the first relates to basic information concerning positions of the employees and their job functions, sums insured selected and maximum amount of cash handled, online money transfers or stock handled by any one employee.

The other section focuses on the system of checks and balances employed by the business such as background checks for new employees, internal controls and systems of audit, the number of signatories required to authorize payments, regularity of bank reconciliation statements, frequency of books audits, obtaining satisfactory written references from former employers and the past accidents experience.

A COMMON MISCONCEPTION

My employees are trustworthy, highly dedicated and they wouldn't steal from me!

This may be the case, but beware of an employee that works long hours and rarely takes long vacations as this could be a potential sign of fraudulent activity. While this employee may appear to be highly dedicated, he or she may be trying to avoid a replacement employee from discovering how the records are being manipulated.

Another sign may be an employee that refuses to delegate work, try to work at home or during off business hours, or even decline a promotion to avoid other employees from reviewing their work.

An employee that is committing theft may go to great lengths to avoid having other employees assist or review their work in order to hide and continue with their fraudulent activities

Recent research findings and developing trends relating to employee fraud risks!

It is estimated that the typical organization loses 5% of revenues each year due to fraud. If applied to the

SECTION 2

THE FIDELITY
GUARANTEE
INSURANCE POLICY

2014 estimated Gross World Product, this translates to a potential projected occupational fraud loss of nearly USD3.7 trillion worldwide. Asset misappropriation is by far the most common of occupational fraud, consistently occurring in more than 83% of all cases reported. These schemes tended to cause a median loss of USD125,000 per scheme.

A global study published in 2011 found that the typical profile of a fraudster is someone that is a male, 36 to 45 years of age, has been employed by a business for more than 10 years, holds a senior management position, works in a finance or finance related role and is in collusion with another perpetrator. Interestingly, it was also estimated that fraud takes longer to detect in emerging economies, for instance it takes on average 5 years for fraud to be discovered in Asia, in contrast to North America where the average is 4.2 years, Western Europe 3.7 and South America averages 2.1.

Examining the association between fraud and a weakened economy, a survey conducted during the 2008-2009 financial crisis showed that more than half the respondents indicated that the number of frauds has increased compared to 2007-2008 period. Additionally, 49 per cent observed an increase in the dollar amount lost to fraud during the same period.

The affliction of increased financial strain due to financial crisis can have an effect on the business as well as individuals. Incidents of fraud will increase as companies shed staff, moderate expenditure and inevitably overlook internal controls. Such measures lead to heightened feelings of vulnerability and negativity which may in turn allow individuals to justify previously inconceivable acts.

Case Studies

The following claims scenarios highlight the range of potential accidents that could arise in the normal course of business.

CASE 1: A payroll clerk creates a ghost employee who receives a salary. The payroll clerk has access to the ghost employee bank account and pockets the funds.

CASE 2: A cashier is caught giving friends a discount at the register and charging for fewer items than these people actually bought.

CASE 3: An IT manager at an accounting firm pays his IT supplier overinflated prices for IT equipment and services in order to receive a large financial kick back

SECTION 2

THE FIDELITY
GUARANTEE
INSURANCE POLICY

The Fire Insurance Policy

(Fire and Special Perils policy / Property Insurance policy)

Fires and natural disasters and are major risks that can have an instantaneous and destructive effect on a business or even an entire economy, costing business dearly in terms of lost revenue and opportunities which can sometimes be irreversible.

While the number of fires may have been falling in recent years, the increase in large scale fires has been increasing.

Likewise, natural disasters such as earthquakes, floods and tsunamis can have devastating impact when they occur, shutting down most activity in the affected area which may spread beyond that area as customers or suppliers are hit by the shutdown and many businesses that are far away will also suffer. There is a good chance that many of those, which might have been marginal to begin with, will just never start up again.

SECTION 2

THE FIRE INSURANCE POLICY

Who is this policy suitable for?

This policy is recommended for owners or financiers or leaseholders or tenants of residential and commercial property.

All movable and immovable property can be insured including buildings, plant and machinery, furniture, fixtures, fittings, personal effects, office equipment, property held in trust or on commission, stocks and stock in progress, stocks at suppliers or customer's premises, machinery temporarily removed from the premises for repairs and other contents.

Cover description

The most basic fire policy would be limited to cover loss or damage to property against fire and lightning accidents. However, typically nowadays, a fire policy will include a myriad of additional perils, referred to as special or allied perils, and may include some or all of the following:

- Explosion of domestic boiler plant
- Aircraft and parts dropped therefrom
- cyclone, typhoon and tornado
- Impact by rail or road vehicle belonging to third parties
- Bursting or overflowing of water tanks or apparatus
- Leakage form automatic sprinkler installation

A term notably used regularly in the insurance industry is FLEXA, this refers to four basic perils grouped together namely, fire, lightning, explosion and falling aircraft or parts thereof. So if this term is encountered just know that the policy provides this basic coverage.

What does it pay for?

The policy indemnifies the Insured for the direct costs associated with the replacement, rebuild or repair of buildings and contents insured caused by fire or other named perils and the damage associated with firefighting. The basis for compensation depends on whether the policy wording stipulates the use of the Replacement Value or Actual Cash Value calculation.

Possible policy extensions

For extra premium, the policy can be extended to include perils that are excluded from the basic policy such as burglary, removal of debris following an accident, liability towards third parties, strikes, riots, civil commotion, sabotage and terrorism, architect and consulting engineers' fees, forest fires, spontaneous combustion, business interruption and many others depending on the requirement of the Insured.

Acts of nature such as storms, tempests, earthquakes, floods, hurricanes and tsunamis can be added for a pre-specified limit of indemnity but occasionally full value cover is agreed to by insurers in parts of the world that don't experience frequent disasters of this nature.

General exclusions

The policy will not pay for loss or damage due to war and war like operations, radioactive contamination or nuclear perils, pollution and contamination, electrical or mechanical breakdown and consequential loss.

The property insured must be in operation and not under construction for the duration of the policy otherwise such property may be excluded from coverage.

The policy will exclude a certain amount which the Insured shall bear referred to as the policy excess or the deductible.

Setting the sum insured

The sum insured should represent the actual value of the property to be insured noting that insuring for values higher than the actual value gives no advantage to the Insured.

Two common methods for calculating the sum insured are briefly outlined below:

The Reinstatement Value Method

The Insured must specify the amount that it would cost to fully rebuild the insured property after a destructive loss. This method prevents the deduction of depreciation and the insurer will pay the cost of repair or replacement in compensation subject to the ceiling of the sum insured (new for old).

Do not use this method for setting the sum insured for stocks or inventory.

The Market Value Method

Unlike the first method, this method allows for the deduction of depreciation on current replacement value of the asset for the number of years it has been in use to arrive at market value.

Additionally, insurance policies can also be issued on declaration basis in instances where the stock in trade undergoes wide fluctuation in value from month to month.

Policy premium calculation

Since fire is the major peril insured against by this policy, it would be advantageous if business premises are near a fire hydrant or fire station. This may not be an issue in urban areas, but in more remote or rural areas, the distance may be greater, impacting the cost of insurance.

An alarm system, smoke detectors, carbon monoxide detectors, automatic sprinklers or other security features will generally result in a discount and help reduce insurance premium.

Premiums are based on the type of occupancy, physical features, values at risk and the requirement of additional covers.

A premium rate per one thousand dollar of the sum insured will be multiplied by the total sums insured deduced by any of the methods mentioned above to arrive at the annual policy premium.

What information do the insurers need to be told in an insurance application?

The scope of information sought by insurers is normally driven by the type of operation the Insured is engaged in and the perils selected in addition to the fire and lightning risks which make up the standard cover.

The Insured should provide information concerning past accidents, age and size of premises, building type of construction, type of business occupying the premises, nature of the goods stored, business carried out in neighboring premises, fire warning and fighting apparatus, ownership of the building, and an itemized list of the property and contents to be covered clearly highlighting whether the cover will be on Reinstatement or Actual Value basis.

If a survey by a risk engineer is conducted, the insurers will review survey report allowing them to assess the quality of risk and to estimate the amount of potential damage to property. In addition, the report may recommend measures aimed at reduction of the probability of loss occurrences.

> ## A COMMON MISCONCEPTION
>
> *Smoke alarms provide enough protection!*
>
> Unfortunately, too often, battery operated smoke alarms fail to function because the batteries are dead or have been removed.
>
> Smoke alarms may be good at saving lives by providing a warning system but can do nothing to extinguish a growing fire or prevent it spreading out.

Recent research findings and developing trends relating to major causes of property losses!

The world is witnessing ever evolving globalization of trade and manufacturing, increasing dependence on robotics, higher concentrations in values and emerging high value risks all of which have contributed to ever higher values and risks.

Globally, fire is the top cause of property insurance claims in terms of both number and values, a study released in 2014 has shown.

The NFPA in the USA has defined the total cost of fires in the United States in 2008, at an estimated USD310 Billion, or roughly 2 % of U.S. gross domestic product, in 2009 this had increased to USD331 Billion or 2.3% of GDP.

During 2007-2011, U.S. local fire departments responded to an estimated average of 22,600 fires per year that were started by lightning and caused USD451 million in direct property damage per year.

Warehouses present special challenges for fire protection, U.S. fire departments responded to an estimated average of 1,210 fires in warehouse properties per year (excluding refrigerated or cold storage) between 2009 -2013. These fires caused an annual average of USD155 million in direct property damage, three civilian deaths, and 19 civilian injuries.

Case Studies

The following claims scenarios highlight the range of potential accidents that could arise in the normal course of business.

CASE 1: Large fire partially destroyed a packaging factory which had been built to recent modern standards of safety and protection. The fire appears to have started as a result of an act of arson but police investigation did not lead to any suspects or legal action. Repairs will be costing the owners millions of dollars and lasting for up to 6 months to complete.

CASE 2: After a fire, a high street department store built in the mid-twenties and valued at hundreds of millions of dollars was declared a total loss. The fire started in the staff canteen when gas leak in one of the cookers caused an explosion. The building was equipped with all the necessary fire detection and fighting equipment except automatic sprinklers.

CASE 3: A multi-storey office building used its basement floor as a storage area. There was so much office files and other contents stacked in the store that they almost touched the lighting fixtures in the ceiling. One day the lights were accidently left switched on causing some plastic folders to catch fire because of the directly overhead hot lamp. Fire was confined to the basement area but before the fire fighters arrived, black noxious smoke had spread through the ventilation system to the floors above.

26

The Group Life Insurance Policy

(Term Life insurance / death in service benefit)

Employee benefits, other than salary, include a broad range of benefits that businesses can provide to their employees. Some of these benefits are required by law, such as workers compensation and health insurance, social security and unemployment insurance. However, certain other fringe benefits are provided at the discretion of the business owner ranging from paid vacations, stock ownership plans and profit sharing to life insurance.

Families facing a sudden loss of income due to the unexpected loss of a homemaker often turn to relatives and friends, government agencies or charity for financial support.

Death and disability are low probability events but they involve significant costs if they occur, the alternative would be relying on savings to cushion the impact of these events which would be difficult, if not impossible, for most families.

SECTION 2

THE GROUP LIFE INSURANCE POLICY

In today's competitive environment with tighter budgets and fewer human resources, every dollar and every effort counts, particularly when it comes to attracting and retaining top talent.

Employer paid-for life insurance is one way of providing employee benefits and rewards as it can be done at low cost.

Who is the policy suitable for?

Group life insurance can be designed for associations, societies and businesses in any trade. It allows employees (in the policy referred to them as members) to enjoy group benefits at low cost.

Most insurers require that a group is composed of at least four members otherwise they would insist on the purchase of individual policies.

The policy may be employer paid for, employee paid for (voluntary) or a combination of the two (contributory).

Cover description

Group life insurance is usually set up as Term Life insurance which means the policy will have an end date coinciding with the normal retirement age for employees.

It is by far the most common form of life insurance available and is often referred to as temporary insurance or pure insurance (meaning no built-in investment element) offering only a death benefit pay out. Cover is usually available on 24-hour worldwide basis.

What does it pay for?

In the event of premature death, insurers make a lump sum pay out to the member's designated beneficiary or beneficiaries (perhaps family or next of kin) using these proceeds for instance to pay for rent, mortgage, school or college tuition fees among other things.

Possible policy extensions

Typically policies may be extended to include additional benefits at additional premium charges for any of the following:

- total and permanent disability due to any cause
- a portability provision enabling eligible employees to continue a certain level of their group coverage when their employment ends
- Conversion, which is the ability to convert to an individual life insurance policy if the member leaves a group scheme
- critical illness cover if the member is diagnosed for cancer, a heart attack or stroke or other conditions allowed by the policy
- additional monthly benefit to the employee's family in the event of death or total and permanent disability
- policies will exclude members that attain a certain age, but it could be raised upon the agreement of the insurer

General exclusions

Exclusions under a group life policy would generally exclude occupations that are considered dangerous such as those in the military or the police or in underground mining, or if engaging in risky pastimes such as parachuting, mountaineering or racing, also excluding those with history of serious health problems and people with unhealthy lifestyles such as smokers or those with overweight problems.

Some policies will not respond if the member's death falls under any of the following circumstances:

- due to alcohol or drug misuse
- involvement in war or terrorism
- suicide or self-inflicted injuries
- gross negligence or a similarly reckless act

Group term life policies do not include any excess or deductible.

Fixing the Sum Insured

The sum insured is typically equal to one or two times the annual salary but members insured under the policy can have different levels of sum insured depending on for instance, the seniority within the organization, for example, managers could have 4 times salary whilst junior staff could have 2 times salary.

Group life policies include useful feature not available in individual life policies and is referred to as a **Non-medical Limit (or a free cover limit)**, this is basically the maximum sum assured that an insurer will insure a member for under a particular scheme without having that member complete a health questionnaire or undergo a medical examination. This amount will vary from scheme to scheme depending on size and the level of benefits. It means that upon joining a group life scheme, a member will be automatically insured up to that agreed limit.

However, the non-medical limits are not normally granted to employees over the age of 65 and a group normally has to have at least 5 members in order to qualify for non-medical limits.

Aggregate amount of sums insured for the all members will form the total sum insured for the group as whole.

Policy premium calculation

For businesses of any size, the cost of providing insurance depends on their age mix of its employees. A business employing many older workers will pay higher life insurance premiums than a business with a younger staff. A relatively small percentage of employees over the age of 65, with high salaries and correspondingly larger amounts of life insurance coverage, can account for a substantial portion of the total premium.

Moreover, groups with low employee turnover or no departures are not necessarily advantageous to employers. If turnover is low, the group will age, mortality will increase and insurance premiums will increase. Many businesses will as a result reduce the amount of coverage for workers that reach age 65 or discontinue the coverage after age 70 to help them control their annual premiums.

Based on the underwriting data received, a unit rate will be deduced for calculation of the premium and is guaranteed until the next annual renewal date.

The unit rate, a per USD 1,000 of coverage for the entire group of employees, will be multiplied by the total sum insured to arrive at the total policy premium. At each subsequent renewal, a rate adjustment may be required to reflect changes in the demographic composition of the group as well as the claims experience.

What information do the insurers need to be told in an insurance application?

The level of detail required for group life schemes is not as complicated as most people tend to think and is in

SECTION 2

THE GROUP LIFE INSURANCE POLICY

fact very simple requiring general information on the employer relating to the nature of the business conducted, normal retirement age and past claims experience.

The rest of the information would be presented in a spread sheet containing the member's age next birthday, the salary multiples on which the benefits are to be based, gender and category of members if more than one category is being submitted for example managers, staff, laborers etc.

For those members over the non-medical limit, individual proposal forms need to be completed by each.

A COMMON MISCONCEPTION

The Group life insurance policy arranged at work is sufficient protection for my family!

That's not totally true. As long as the employee remains in the employment of the employer, cover will be available. However, if the employee leaves or is terminated, the policy stays with the employer and the employee loses that cover.

It is always best practice for the employee to have a separate individual policy other than the group life policy to prevent being exposed to such a situation.

Recent research findings and developing trends on employee benefits

Most employers take part in the competitive landscape for attracting or maintaining employees by offering benefits while there is evidence that larger companies usually offer more in terms of benefits.

Employers that provide a comprehensive benefits package are likely to have an advantage in attracting and retaining employees. When employers were asked in a study about their top employee benefits objectives, employers rated retaining employees as the second most important objective, with 53% stating this is a "very important" objective, this is second to controlling health care related costs. When it comes to life insurance products, the workplace is more often the place where this type of insurance is made available. Employees rely heavily on the workplace for many personal insurance and savings products.

The U.S. Bureau of Labor Statistics reported that 72 per cent of full-time, private industry employees across the US had access to life insurance benefits. And among those who had access, 98 per cent took advantage of the benefit.

Life insurance undoubtedly protects against the financial loss resulting from the untimely death of an income earner or family maker. An academic study predicted that a surviving spouse's standard of living will fall by 44 per cent without life insurance protection. It is especially important for children as their lives can be dramatically affected by the loss of an uninsured parent. In 2009, there were 89.8 million children below the age of 20 in the United States of which 57 per cent (50.8 million) benefited from life insurance policies.

Case Studies

The following claims scenarios highlight the range of potential accidents that could arise in the normal course of business.

CASE 1: A 35 year old managing partner of an accounting firm was in good physical shape when he suddenly felt unwell at work. His left side was numb, his head had dropped and he was incoherent when speaking to his secretary. He was rushed to hospital where he was confirmed of having suffered from stroke.

CASE 2: Jasmine 31, returned home from work with a bad headache and suspecting that she might be getting the flu. Later the same day, she lost consciousness and was rushed to hospital by her husband. She had suffered brain haemorrhage and died that evening without regaining consciousness.

CASE 3: A tourism executive travelled in his off road vehicle to sample some hotels in the Australian outback and accidentally collided with an adult kangaroo. The accident wasn't discovered till the next morning, but he had already succumbed to his injuries and died on the spot.

The Marine Hull and Machinery Insurance Policy

For individuals of substantial net worth, few pastimes offer more pleasure than cruising the oceans in an own boat or yacht. Yacht ownership obviously represents a significant capital investment and entails huge financial vulnerabilities given the unpredictable nature of the weather and the multitude of international maritime laws. The ongoing responsibilities are manifold and could overwhelm even the most diligent yacht owner. Damage or loss to the boat may mean that the owner will potentially suffer a huge financial loss in terms of the repair costs, recovery and lost income.

Commercial vessels are a different ballgame altogether, commercial shipping is the most international of all the trade services and is perilous at the same time, though it has always provided the only really cost effective method of bulk transport over great distances.

SECTION 2

THE MARINE HULL AND MACHINERY INSURANCE POLICY

Continuous advancement in ship construction has meant that ships are carrying ever more cargo and are ever more technically sophisticated, ever more immense, safer and more environmentally friendly.

Accidents are not only undesirable outcomes in themselves to the stakeholders in a ship but they also have a wider negative impact on the supply chain.

Who is the policy suitable for?

This policy is suited for the protection of the interests of ship owners, charterers, shipbuilders and financiers whether for pleasure or commercial use.

Marine vessel examples include boats, ships of all shapes and sizes such as pleasure sail craft, yachts, dinghies, tankers, bulk carriers, barges, tugs, towboats, fishing boats, passenger cruise ships and catamarans.

Cover description

Ships of different types and trades need different consideration when it comes to the scope and terms of hull and machinery insurance policy.

The policy basically insures the vessel and its machinery which would include the hull, its propulsion and power generation machinery, navigation instruments, apparatus, fixture and fittings, installations and annexes whether on the vessel or taken off.

Coverage most commonly includes:

- accidental physical loss or damage
- collision liability or contact with fixed or floating objects

- salvage, general average, sue and labor and legal costs

For example, the policy generally provides protection against loss or damage due to fire, explosion, stranding, sinking, piracy and collision damage to the vessel and its machinery.

What does it pay for?

The policy provides reimbursement following total loss of a vessel, cost of repairing or replacing damaged parts, expenses paid for preventing and minimizing damage, general average contribution (please read the marine cargo section for clarification) and salvage expenses.

Possible policy extensions

More commonly, hull and machinery policies may be extended to include cover for increased value insurance (to cover the additional costs associated with replacing a lost ship), loss of hire, mortgage interest, war, strikes, riots and civil commotions, fuel and stores on-board cover, cash on-board, running down clause (covers negligence of the carrier or the shipper that results in damage to the property of others) and fixed and floating objects cover.

Adding additional perils and extending the policy coverage will entail additional premium charges.

General exclusions

Common exclusions seen in many policies include loss, damage or expense occurring as a result of deliberate and wrongful act of any person, loss of life or injury, costs or wreck removal, liability to cargo owners, use of any weapon of war employing atomic or nuclear fission and or fusion, radioactive contamination, chemical or biochemical or biological or electromagnetic weapons, insolvency or financial default of the vessel owner or operators or charterers, war, strike, riot or civil commotion and terrorism.

A deductible for each and every loss under the policy may be applicable.

Setting the sum insured

In practice the vast majority of hull and machinery policies are on agreed value basis in which the value insured is agreed between the insurer and the Insured and is fixed at a certain amount for hull and machinery and accessories.

Policy premium calculation

When it comes to hull insurance the rate applied is normally fairly static regardless of vessel value, however the rate applied will largely depend on the vessel category, vessel specifications and construction type, engine horsepower, vessel age, cruising or trading range, safety equipment and the mooring type. Age of skipper is not usually a factor determining hull insurance cost.

For a hull and machinery policy, a premium rate per one hundred dollar will be multiplied by the agreed value to arrive at the annual policy premium.

Interestingly, for yachts and leisure boats in particular, the insurers may allow a hull policy to "lay up" or to suspend coverage for specified periods when the vessel is not in use allowing the Insured to benefit from a cut in premium during those days or months when the vessel is not in use.

What information do the insurers need to be told in an insurance application?

Insurance underwriters will require information relating to the purpose the vessel is used for, the operators and managers, the flag, its navigational limits, the desired insured value for the hull and machinery, limit of legal liability and the past accident experience.

Further questions will relate to the specifications of the vessel including its maximum speed, construction, year of build, length, engine specification, passenger and crew capacity and date of condition survey or registration. Some insurers may request information about the skipper.

A COMMON MISCONCEPTION

In circumstances when the Insured has been instructed by the insurer to get a survey, some ship owners think that they have become entitled to get insurance!

Carrying out a survey does not provide an automatic agreement by the insurer to provide insurance cover. In fact the survey findings might be cause for the insurer to refuse to provide cover or may make the offer conditional to the Insured satisfying certain improvements.

Recent research findings and developing trends on major causes of loss

In 2010, the world fleet of seagoing merchant ships consisted of more than 104,000 ships averaging 22 years of age (of no less than 100 Gross Ton in weight), registered

SECTION 2

THE MARINE HULL
AND MACHINERY
INSURANCE POLICY

in over 150 nations and manned by 1.5 million seafarers of virtually every nationality.

Piracy has for some years now grabbed global headlines due to the violence it involves and its economic impact, it is estimated that it impeded the delivery of shipments and increased shipping expenses, costing as a result an estimated USD 6.6 to 6.9 billion annually in global trade according to OBP.

Ransom payments to Somali pirates are estimated to have been between USD339 million and 413 million in the period 2005-2012, according to a report released by The World Bank which focused on Somalia, Djibouti, Ethiopia, Kenya and the Seychelles.

In another annual piracy report, it was shown that 245 piracy incidents were recorded worldwide in 2014 which is a 44% drop since Somali piracy peaked in 2011. Somali pirates were responsible for 11 attacks, all of which were successfully thwarted. Worldwide, 21 vessels were hijacked, 183 were boarded and 13 fired upon.

The drop has been attributed to the adoption of best management practices by vessel owners and crews, armed private security onboard ships, a significant naval presence and the development of onshore security forces.

Hull losses continue to show a general downward trend in total-loss frequency for most vessel types, however, an overall increase has been observed in the percentage of the frequency of heavy weather and grounding related total losses.

Case Studies

The following claims scenarios highlight the range of potential accidents that could arise in the normal course of business.

CASE 1: An Iranian fishing vessel is hijacked in January 2014 by Somali pirates in the red Sea, with 10 man crew consisting of various nationalities. After sending a distress signal, the vessel was boarded by a gang of around eight armed pirates and taken to Gulf of Aden. The same ship had also been attacked in 2011, but had escaped that time.

CASE 2: Late in the evening, the passenger ferry *Sea Smooth* crashed into another passenger ferry called *Lamma IV* off Hong Kong, rupturing its two watertight compartments causing them to quickly fill with water. The *Lamma* capsized with the rear sinking quickly into the sea throwing more than 100 passengers into the water, unprotected, despite the abundance of life-vests on board.

CASE 3: Two cruise ships, The *Norwegian Star* and the *Royal Caribbean Explorer of the Seas* were moored stern-to-stern at the Royal Dockyard in Bermuda. In the afternoon a tremendous storm accompanied with heavy rain and 75mph wind gusts caused the forward moorings of the Norwegian Star to be ripped loose and the ship was blown on a collision course with the otherwise stationary Explorer of the Seas. Both suffered from big dents after the bump.

Useful reading

IMB Piracy & Armed Robbery Map 2016, a live map shows all piracy and armed robbery incidents reported to IMB Piracy Reporting Centre during 2016.

SECTION 2

THE MARINE HULL
AND MACHINERY
INSURANCE POLICY

28

The Inland Transit Insurance Policy

(Goods in Transit)

This policy is very similar to that of marine cargo insurance in terms of the protection that it affords and it is recommended that the Marine Cargo insurance section presented in this book is read before proceeding here.

The basic difference lies in that inland transit covers domestic transits via land conveyances and air shipments. Some of the claims that do occur frequently include inadequate cargo loading, fastening or security, cargo falling off the vehicle during strong braking or a crash, or overturning when negotiating curves in the road.

Marine cargo insurance on the other hand, often provides coverage for international ocean and air shipments including the land connecting conveyance transits.

SECTION 2

THE INLAND TRANSIT INSURANCE POLICY

Who is the policy suitable for?

The policy is mostly purchased by the owners of the merchandise and focuses on providing cover for the contents whilst being carried by vans, pickups, lorries and similar conveyances, whether goods are carried in own vehicles or by professional carriers.

It is also useful for the independent courier or the franchised network-operator and those in the haulage industry providing up to full-value of cover should their customer's materials, goods or cargo be lost, stolen or damaged in transit.

This policy covers loss, destruction or damage to the goods shipped by the seller but not yet received by the purchaser whilst in transit by a lorry, train or any other conveyance licensed to carry goods and whilst temporarily housed in the ordinary course of transit within the territorial limit agreed, caused by named perils or accidental means.

Unlike marine Cargo insurance, warehouse to warehouse coverage is not necessarily covered for Inland Transit policies, though this can be arranged.

Two types of cover can be offered:

1. **An all risks cover**, insuring against all risks of loss or damage to the insured goods whilst in transit by road or rail.

2. **A limited cover**, insuring against loss or damage to the insured goods whilst in transit by road or rail caused by fire, lightning, breakdown of bridges, collision, overturning or derailment. Loss as a result of theft is excluded.

Typically policies can take one of the following forms:

1. **Single transit**
   this policy covers a single transit of cargo from one place to another.

2. **Annual policy**
   covers all transits made by or for the Insured during a 12 months period of insurance. Insurance certificates are issued once shipments are declared as evidence of contract

What does it pay for?

The policy provides protection against the actual costs of replacing goods lost or damaged during transit or while kept in warehousing in the interim period, the costs incurred in trying to minimize loss and expenses involved in inspection.

Possible policy extensions

Generally, policies may be extended at additional premium charges to include loss or damage resulting from, strikes, riots and civil commotion, debris removal, delayed discovery of transit damage(unpacking), damage and loss from unattended vehicles.

General exclusions

There is widely accepted list of excluded perils that excludes all loss or damage resulting from war, strikes, riots and civil commotions, willful misconduct of the Insured, dishonesty of any employee or servant of the Insured, inherent vice or nature of insured items, ordinary leakage, loss in weight or volume or wear and tear of insured items, insufficiency or unsuitability of packing

SECTION 2

THE INLAND TRANSIT INSURANCE POLICY

or preparation of the insured items, any weapon of war or any weapon employing atomic or nuclear fission or fusion or other like reaction or radioactive force or matter.

The policy is not designed to cover the loss or damage to goods while handled by market traders or door to door salespeople neither will it cover the loss of money or documents while in transit.

A deductible for each and every loss under the policy may be applicable.

Setting the sum insured

Generally, the policy limit should reflect the maximum value being shipped in any one conveyance. When choosing the amount, the following should be kept in mind:

- Transit policies typically value goods at the invoice cost plus freight charges plus an advance of between 10 and 20 per cent to cover expenses incurred during shipping that are unknown at the time of shipping.

- For an exporter, profit is generally already included in the invoice cost. An importer may want to select an advance valuation that includes a profit margin, and may also want to include coverage for duty and taxes, if any.

In the case of the Single transit policy, the sum insured is the value of the goods transited.

However, in the case of the Annual transit Policy, the sum insured is that of the value of goods estimated to be carried in a 12 months period.

Typically, for the annual policy, a pre-agreed maximum limit for insured value per any one consignment or vehicle or conveyance will apply. The insurance company will have to price in advance any carrying exceeding this limit on case by case basis.

Policy premium calculation

Premium rates may vary depending on type of goods, the limit per conveyance, the frequency of sending and the coverage type required.

For a single transit policy, a premium rate per one hundred dollar will be multiplied by the value of goods transited to arrive at the policy premium.

For an annual policy, a provisional annual premium is calculated by multiplying a premium rate per one hundred dollar of the sum insured by the estimated annual carrying. Premium is paid upfront and subject to adjustment based on the actual carrying declared at the end of policy period.

What information do the insurers need to be told in an insurance application?

The underwriting information requirement may include information relating to type of goods carried, type of packaging, size of carrying vehicles, the limit per conveyance, where the vehicle is kept overnight, the estimated annual value of insured goods, geographical limits, the coverage required and past claims experience. The susceptibility of the goods to damage, theft and pilferage is vital important information.

The Insured has to indicate whether the limited or the extended type of coverage is required so that the insurance offer is prepared accordingly.

SECTION 2

THE INLAND TRANSIT INSURANCE POLICY

A COMMON MISCONCEPTION

We have an all risks Goods in Transit policy that provides protection against everything!

Whilst the general intention of an all risks policy is to provide the widest cover possible without naming a single cause of loss, no policy will ever provide cover against everything.

The Insured must ensure that the policy wording is reviewed frequently after taking due care and consideration of the demands of the business and past losses suffered.

Recent research findings and developing trends on major causes of truck accidents

The land transport sector in the European Union encompasses the use of many different commercial vehicles including lorries and vans and is characterized by a large number of small companies, predominantly with fewer than 10 drivers and self-employed drivers, although there are marked differences between the different countries in the union.

According to a Danish study of road traffic accidents, there are certain features of heavy good vehicles that increase the accident risk of trucks:

- the dimensions of trucks
- the reduced braking and evasive abilities of trucks can contribute to collisions and overturning

Another scientific study into European truck accident causation analyzed 624 accidents, found that human error was the main contributor to road accidents (85.2%) while factors such as weather, infrastructure conditions or technical failures of vehicles played a minor role.

Furthermore, an Austrian study found that 40% of all heavy goods vehicles had insufficient or improper or no cargo securing at all. And about 70% of the drivers had never been trained professionally in cargo safety.

Case Studies

The following claims scenarios highlight the range of potential accidents that could arise in the normal course of business.

CASE 1: A lorry fails to reduce speed sufficiently when exiting the motorway causing the heavily laden vehicle to skid off at the corner and crashes down the slip road embankment. The cargo is a shipment of television sets worth USD 250,000 is scattered all over the motorway. The goods are considered total loss.

CASE 2: Workers of an express courier delivering a large brand new heavy duty copying machine accidentally dropped the machine to the ground from a height of approximately half a meter while unloading it from the truck. The machine suffers damage to its steel frame which wasn't visible from the outside. The damage is discovered a day later when maintenance personnel were called in to solve a problem with excessive noise.

CASE 3: Half the stock of a delivery van carrying cartons of cigarettes is stolen when the driver leaves the truck parked on back alley while he went for lunch nearby. The police were never able to recover the stolen stock.

SECTION 2

THE INLAND
TRANSIT INSURANCE
POLICY

The Key Person Insurance Policy

(Key Man insurance)

From small firms to large companies, almost every business has some form of insurance to protect its physical assets, like its manufacturing facilities, stock inventory and office premises to mitigate potential financial losses through natural and man-made disasters.

But it's widely conceived that the most important asset of a company is it's people especially those individuals whose talents, expertise, skills, ideas, vision and business contacts drive the business and provide it with competitive advantage.

Replacing a key person takes time and money and could cost the business valuable clients during the transition. It's probably the last thing on the mind of a most business owners, but it's among one of the most important.

Thinking ahead and preparing for the unexpected is what makes a business successful. Preparation for the unexpected events of the death or the disability of a key person is crucial and is more so for a small business or a start-up.

SECTION 2

THE KEY PERSON INSURANCE POLICY

Who is the policy suitable for?

Business can insure against the financial loss that it would suffer if a key person died or were totally and permanently disabled.

The general rule for deciding whether or not a person is a key person in the business is to simply assess whether the business would financially suffer a great loss or even shut down if this person is unable to come to work.

The key person may be an executive, principal shareholder, a senior scientist, a partner or a particularly successful salesperson.

Cover description

Key person insurance is life insurance, technically called a Term Life policy, which in its most basic form provides a capital benefit if a key person dies regardless of the cause of death. However, more often than not, such policies will include coverage against total and permanent disability due to any cause whether accidental or illness.

Key limitations to coverage may include:

- the person being insured must be between ages 18 and 55
- the policy can be maintained until the insured reaches age 62

What does it pay for?

Key person protection is designed to pay out a lump sum on the total and permanent disability or death of the insured key person.

The business is the beneficiary under the policy. It can use the insurance proceeds to:

- cover expenses to recruit, hire and train a successor
- pay off debt and deal with creditors
- alleviate lenders' concerns about business's financial health
- reassure customers, employees and investors that the business is still viable

Possible policy extensions

Cover can be extended to include critical illness insurance, which pays out a lump sum of money should the Insured be diagnosed with having one of a list of specified critical illnesses.

Such an extension to the policy cover will entail additional premium charges.

General exclusions

Exclusions are identical to those relating to regular life policies and would mostly exclude employment or service that is considered high risk such as military personnel and underground miners and would exclude risky activities or past times such as parachuting, mountaineering or racing, also exclude people with history of serious health problems and unhealthy lifestyles such as smokers or those with overweight problems.

Some policies will not pay out if the life insured's death falls under the following circumstances:

- due to alcohol or drug misuse
- involvement in war or terrorism
- suicide or self-inflicted injury
- gross negligence or a similarly reckless act
- war whether declared or not

Setting the sum insured

Whilst it is very difficult to value intangible risk factors such as the potential loss of goodwill and distinctive client relationships, the cover required is usually determined by the size of the business and the person that is to be insured. Budget will no doubt be a factor.

A thorough analysis must be made to estimate the amount of turnover attributed to the key person, the time frame until sales can be recovered, cost of recruitment, training and the replacement.

The most common method is to include a salary multiple, for instance 5 to 10 times the key employees' annual salary including bonuses. Age will be factored in when the multiple is considered by the insurer.

The sum insured can range between few hundred thousand dollars and millions of dollars.

Start-up companies with no revenue will be limited in the size of the sum insured they can select when insuring their key persons.

Policy premium calculation

The size of the premium rate set by the insurers is affected by important factors relating to the age and health of the key person, the unique skills or talents the key person has and make him indispensable, the future business endeavors, the liquidity of business assets and the reputation of both the company and the key person.

This is a simple enough calculation whereby the deduced premium rate per one thousand dollar of the sum insured will be multiplied by the total sum insured to arrive at the annual policy premium.

What information do the insurers need to be told in an insurance application?

Insurers need to be satisfied that the proposer stands to lose from the death of the life assured.

For larger sums assured, independent financial evidence will be needed to illustrate the need for the cover, for example, audited accounts and a written statement from the company accountant.

Medical guidelines for underwriting key person insurance are usually the same as for any personal life insurance plan.

The insurer will want to know the nature of the business, when the company was started, net worth of the company, is the key person an owner of the business and are all key people will be insured. Insurers will also want to see that all key persons or owners of the company are insured. It's a red flag to them if any key persons or owners aren't being insured, unless they are uninsurable (for example, ill health or over the age of 75).

SECTION 2

THE KEY PERSON INSURANCE POLICY

A COMMON MISCONCEPTION

The purpose of the policy is to provide funds to help the principals buy out each other's share in the business in the event one of them dies or is disabled, i.e. succession planning!

This policy is not suitable for this purpose. The Key Person policy is both owned and paid for by the business where as business succession insurance could be self-owned or cross owned by the principals.

The main purpose of Key Person insurance is the protection against potential loss of sales, goodwill, credit rating and related expenses and insurance is only available where there is a realistic and inherent risk of loss to the business.

Recent research findings and developing trends relating to business failures induced by the loss of a key person

Taking the U.S. economy as an example and to illustrate the importance of contingency planning for small businesses following the demise of a founder, consider that there are 6 million businesses in active operation in the United States employing one or more employees. Of those, 3.8 million have four or fewer employees. Next, there are approximately a million companies with five to nine employees, 600,000 businesses with 10 to 19 employees, and 500,000 companies with 20 to 99 employees.

Research shows that the loss of a key person was among the top causes of small business bankruptcies. The death of founding entrepreneurs causes reduction of on average 60% of a firm's sales and cuts jobs by approximately 17%.

Businesses that lost their founders due to death have 20% lower survival rates two years after the death compared to other businesses where the founder is still alive.

Case Studies

The following claims scenarios highlight the range of potential accidents that could arise in the normal course of business.

CASE 1: Sarah, the main shareholder of a manufacturing business, employing 27 workers, spends long hours doing much of the work herself. She deals with many of the business's clients on a personal basis. The business has recently received a big loan from the bank to help in the rapid expansion plans of the business. Unfortunately, soon afterwards, Sarah gets killed in an accident while on a kayaking trip.

CASE 2: A computer maintenance company employing 4 workers was doing quite well when the owner aged 53 suddenly died of a heart attack. The company was wound up 14 months after his death. Former employees insist that the company would have gone on and grown further had the owner survived. None of the employees then was able to take on the task of running the business.

CASE 3: The founder of a high end furniture-making business underwent for 10 months medical treatment for brain tumor, during this time the business which employed 9 workers almost ground to a halt. Fortunately, the tumor was removed and after fully recovering he returned to work to try and regain the lost customers and goodwill that the business had suffered.

SECTION 2

THE KEY PERSON
INSURANCE POLICY

The Equipment Breakdown Insurance Policy

(Boiler and Machinery insurance / Machinery Breakdown insurance)

The speed at which business is done nowadays makes any downtime a critical issue. Businesses, more than ever rely on fragile electronic components that are subject to frequent and costly breakdowns as do traditional mechanical equipment.

Reliance on new technologies and equipment has actually led to a greater probability that a business critical system could fail. Even with expert installation and regular maintenance, equipment does breakdown and mechanical or electrical failure can essentially shut down a business.

Businesses need to protect critical equipment and plan for contingencies. Whilst the ubiquitous property policies only cover damage to equipment from external accidental causes such as fire, flood, hail, windstorm, and

SECTION 2

THE EQUIPMENT BREAKDOWN INSURANCE POLICY

earthquake, they do not however cover damage against accidental electrical failure and mechanical breakdown.

Who is the policy suitable for?

Any type of business that could face potentially significant disruption due to stoppage resulting from accidental breakdown to their fixed (not mobile) equipment is a suitable customer for this policy.

A sample of such equipment may include, food production plants, pumps, lathes, ventilation equipment, transformers, electrical switchgears, pressure vessels or boilers, elevators and escalators.

There is an endless variety of businesses that rely on such equipment including hotels, restaurants, dry cleaners, dairies, bakeries, car washers, bowling centres, foundries, printing press, cold storage, canned food manufacturing, power generation stations and plastic toy manufacturing. This is just a sample of businesses that use equipment and production lines.

Cover description

Typically, policy covers sudden accidental electrical, electronic and mechanical breakdown from internal causes during operation or at rest. This is an all risks policy, the general intention of which is to cover the widest range of unnamed risks not specifically excluded under the policy.

The reader should contrast the scope of this coverage with that of a manufacturer's product warranty which may only cover breakdown caused by faulty materials or workmanship, therefore operator error would not be covered.

Equipment Inspection

Since loss prevention is most important, the insurance company usually provides an inspection service to the Insured's equipment. This is important and in some cases mandatory by state or municipal authorities of the Insured to subscribe to annual inspections for some types of equipment which some insurers are able and willing to perform as part of their underwriting process.

Such inspections and consultative risk assessments not only assist the Insured in complying with regulations by identifying potential hazards and taking preventive measures but also provide the Insured with jurisdictionally required certification and reports for boilers and pressure vessels of service status and function.

Common accidents the policy provides cover against include, breakdown, explosion, collapse, falling, impact, collision, machine tearing apart due to centrifugal force, electrical short circuits, motor burnout, power surge, obstruction or the entry of foreign bodies into machinery. Also, boiler overheating, cracking, sagging or bulging.

What does it pay for?

Typically, this policy may be extended at additional premium charges to include deterioration of stock, express freight, air freight, holiday and overtime pay, hiring of temporary plant, damage to owner's surrounding property, third party liability and loss of profit resulting from equipment breakdown.

Possible policy extensions

Generally, policies may be extended to include, equipment business interruption, deterioration of stock, express freight, air freight, holiday and overtime pay, hiring of temporary plant, owner's surrounding property, third party liability and equipment breakdown Loss of Profit.

Adding additional perils to the policy cover will entail additional premium charges.

General exclusions

Exclusions generally apply to loss or damage resulting from fire and allied perils, gradually developing flaws, defects, cracks or partial fractures, deterioration of or wearing out of any part of any machine, willful act or negligence, loss of use, business interruption, contractual liabilities, overload experiments, tests or abnormal operating conditions and any damage recoverable under manufacturer warranty.

A deductible for each and every claim may be applicable under the policy.

Setting the sum insured

Typically the sum insured should be equal to the cost of replacement of the machinery with new one of the same specification which would represent the present day purchase price of a similar new machine including all incidental expenses such as erection costs, custom duties, freight and insurance and handling charges.

Policy premium calculation

Discounts can be forthcoming if formal maintenance arrangements or contracts are in compliance with manufacturers recommended maintenance schedule and strictly following the manufacturers operating instructions to keep the equipment in good working order.

Additionally, stand-by facility, availability of spare parts, compliance with all statutory obligations, regulations and safety requirement imposed by any authority and a favorable claims experience are added advantages.

The total replacement value for all the machinery insured forms the base of calculating the premium.

A premium rate per one thousand dollar will be multiplied by the total replacement value to arrive at the annual policy premium.

What information do the insurers need to be told in an insurance application?

The most basic information requirement will include manufacturer information and reputation, description of the machinery including specifications, the repair facilities and the extent of maintenance or servicing, the general housekeeping and working environment, the extent of obsolescence of the equipment, availability of replacement parts, territorial location and details concerning past accidents and claims experience.

If business interruption or contingent business interruption are required additional coverage, the Insured will have to provide details of contingency planning, bottlenecks, internal backup alternatives, the percentage capacity at which the machinery is running, estimated repair times and availability of similar businesses nearby for outsourcing.

A COMMON MISCONCEPTION

A complete and detailed list of equipment is required for this policy!

SECTION 2

THE EQUIPMENT BREAKDOWN INSURANCE POLICY

Some business owners think that they must prepare a detailed schedule of all their machinery including specifications and serial numbers in order that the policy covers all of their property.

Overwhelmingly, insurers nowadays will accept a generalized description of the plants and machinery installed on the premises.

Recent research findings and developing trends on the costs of machinery breakdown

Breakdowns are the most common causes of efficiency loss especially in manufacturing. Eliminating unplanned downtime is critical to improving overall equipment efficiency.

Types of downtime can be divided into planned and unplanned downtime. Unplanned downtime accounts for only about 10% of all downtime and is much harder to predict and therefore the consequences may be more damaging to the business, physically and financially than many occurrences of planned downtime.

A 2014 global insurance claims study estimates that claims for equipment breakdown come only second to fire claims in terms of volume but ranks third after fire and earthquake in terms of aggregate claims values.

When equipment is down, it impacts two particular groups financially. There is the economic impact to the investor who may be paying interest on the capital invested in that equipment and there is also the operator who benefits from the revenue generated from running that piece of equipment.

Business insiders estimate that the annual costs to industry from downtime caused by power surges and other related anomalies have ranged from USD30 billion to USD200 billion.

Additionally, looking at the IT sector, it has been reported by Dunn & Bradstreet, that 59% of Fortune 500 companies experience at least 1.6 hours of downtime per week. The labor part of downtime costs for businesses this size would be USD 896,000 weekly, translating into more than USD 46 million per year.

Unfortunately, there isn't enough research done on this topic, however, piecing together the different sets of data on equipment breakdown claims, it transpires that 80% of the claims arise from electrical or air conditioning equipment including refrigeration equipment, electrical distribution equipment including breaker panels, transformers and meters.

The most common causes of equipment breakdown include, operator error, improper start up, lubrication failure, failure of safety devices, foreign material and electricity supply line surges.

Case Studies

The following claims scenarios highlight the range of potential accidents that could arise in the normal course of business.

CASE 1: A shopping mall had to shut down for six days for health and safety reasons whilst repairs were undertaken to the air conditioning system resulting from the failure in the air conditioning condenser. The mall owners lost six days of rental income from more than 50 of their retail tenants.

SECTION 2

THE EQUIPMENT
BREAKDOWN
INSURANCE POLICY

CASE 2: An office building was left without elevators for a whole day after electric arching destroyed main electrical panels leading to disruption to tenants and visitors alike.

CASE 3: The PBX (Private Branch Exchange) system installed in the office of a large law firm that manages phone lines and control incoming and outgoing calls had suddenly gone out of order. The sensitive circuitry had burnt out due to electrical disturbance caused by what is referred to as harmonic distortion created by nonlinear power loads, an issue that befalls most digital equipment.

31

The Medical Malpractice Insurance Policy

(Medical Professional Liability)

Where the medical profession is concerned, the ultimate aim of tort law and the courts is to deter injury and compensate injured victims thereby serving justice and providing a safety net for victims.

If a victim can prove that a medical provider didn't provide the "standard of care" expected for the diagnosis of the medical condition or the treatment or the rehabilitation of the patient, then a medical malpractice claim may arise as a result of what may be considered an act of negligence. The "standard of care" referred to above, means what a reasonably prudent medical provider would have or would have not done for a similar condition.

Failure to diagnose, misdiagnosis, surgical errors, prescription errors, birth injuries, nursing home abuse by providers such as hospitals, doctors, nurses, technicians and other professionals are typical examples.

SECTION 2

THE MEDICAL
MALPRACTICE
INSURANCE POLICY

Usually, medical malpractice legal cases are neither easy nor fast to prove and the legal process can be a long and complicated one not to mention the expense and stress for the medical provider and the victim alike.

Medical providers and physicians must always monitor professional risks and weigh their potential for loss.

Who is the policy suitable for?

This policy is intended to cover a wide variety of medical service providers both on individual as well as group level. Complete facilities could be insured under a single group policy.

A wide variety of service providers can be covered including dental centres, laboratories, pharmacies, hospitals, multi-specialty clinics, urgent care facilities and rehabilitation centres.

Policy coverage is available for surgeons, general practitioners, nurses, paramedics, students, volunteers and many others involved in availing medical services or assistance.

Cover description

The medical malpractice policy provides cover against claims made by third parties for bodily injury, mental injury, illness, disease or death caused by any negligent act, error or omission committed by the Insured.

Claims-made basis is the most common form for this type of policy, meaning cover is available for claims arising from incidents that both occur and are reported to the insurance company while the policy is in force.

What does it pay for?

The medical malpractice insurance policy will indemnify the Insured for the legal costs incurred in defending an action, expenses of expert witnesses and any subsequent out of court settlements or damages awarded by the court against the Insured.

Possible policy extensions

Generally, policies may be extended at additional premium charges to include public liability, cover for claims against the Insured due to the dishonesty of individual partners or directors or employees or self-employed freelancers directly contracted to the Insured and under his supervision.

Cover may also be granted for claims arising from the principal's previous business.

Other less common extensions include cover for loss of money or goods belonging to or held in trust by the Insured due to employee fraud or dishonesty.

General exclusions

Typically these policies exclude coverage of illegal conduct, intentional misconduct, sexual improprieties, hospital or laboratory administration and records alteration, any pollution or contamination including noise, electromagnetic fields, radiation and radio waves.

Any act, breach, omission or infringement deliberately, spitefully, dishonestly or recklessly committed, condoned or ignored.

The supply, manufacture, sale, installation or maintenance of any product is also a standard exclusion.

A deductible for each and every loss may be applicable under the policy.

Setting the liability limit

Most individual policies are nowadays standardized by way of asking the Insured to select the required limit of indemnity per any one occurrence from a pre-defined table of indemnity limits. The selected any-one-occurrence limit will coincide with a pre-defined annual aggregate of claims.

Business entities will determine the required limit of indemnity based on their past claims resulting in that both the per-occurrence limit and the aggregate limits being exponentially larger than that for professional individuals.

Any claims paid will reduce the amount of the applicable aggregate limit available for any other claim.

Policy premium calculation

The base of calculating the premium is the estimated annual turnover of the clinic, hospital or whatever the medical provider maybe.

A premium rate per one thousand dollar will be multiplied by the total turnover to arrive at the annual policy premium. More commonly especially for individual policies, the premium payable is preset for a particular limit of indemnity and physician's specialty enabling the individual to make his selection from a brochure or leaflet. Physicians who are members of a group often can negotiate for better rates.

Some specialties are considered higher-risk because patients are more likely to have complications or because they have more serious illnesses or injuries. Emergency medicine, anaesthesia, orthopaedics, neurosurgery, obstetrics and gynaecology are all specialties with premiums that tend to be higher than average. Moreover, the location of a physician's practice can have a significant impact on the premium level, as certain regions may be more litigious than others.

Unlike most other insurance policies, the Insured may be also able to select policy terms longer than the standard 12 months term for periods of up to 5 years locking-in some favorable discounts.

What information do the insurers need to be told in an insurance application?

The information will be collected in a proposal form completed by the Insured detailing past accidents and claims experience, type of medical services offered, estimated gross annual turnover, name of principles, directors and their professional qualifications, the estimated number of volunteers and students in any given year, category of professionals employed and the limit of Indemnity required.

The Insured may be asked to detail the procedures in place for dealing with patient complaints and the extent of patient records keeping.

A COMMON MISCONCEPTION

The Samaritan act!

If you thought that treatment voluntarily administered by a doctor at the scene of a road accident at which he is present by chance would never be cause for a legal suit, think again!

SECTION 2

THE MEDICAL
MALPRACTICE
INSURANCE POLICY

> Medical staff would still need to have the cover of medical malpractice policy to protect their legal liabilities even for voluntary acts of kindness and unexpected real life situations.

Recent research findings and developing trends on medical malpractice claims

The exponential increase evident over the past 25 years in the payouts for medical malpractice suits has promoted defensive practices by physicians to reduce the threat of legal action. Such practices included ordering of multiple tests and sometimes unnecessary referral to other specialists as noted in a study conducted in the UK, similar attitude has been observed in other western economies as well.

The frequency of medical malpractice suits in the USA however, has been on a steady decline since 2001 due to the high cost of bringing action against a provider or a physician.

A research study in 2013 reported that most malpractice suits against primary care doctors in the USA, UK, Australia, France and Canada were for missed or delayed diagnoses. Missed diagnosis frequently caused severe patient harm, claimed the lives of 160,000 patients a year and led to the biggest total payouts and related mainly to meningitis cases in children, cancer and myocardial infarction in adults.

In the USA, medical negligence was the third leading cause of death behind heart disease and cancer according to study published in the Journal of the American Medical Association (JAMA) in 2000.

Case Studies

The following claims scenarios highlight the range of potential accidents that could arise in the normal course of business.

CASE 1: An elderly patient required an operation to stop the flow of bleeding from brain to skull. A CAT scan is performed and indicates that the bleeding was happening on the left side of the brain. The surgeon incorrectly started the procedure by drilling a hole on the wrong side of the patient's skull. The surgeon somehow discovers the error, closes the first hole and drills a second to the correct side of the patient's head this time.

CASE 2: A mother experiences an umbilical cord prolapse during child delivery operation and unfortunately as a result the baby suffers brain damage because the doctor failed to act immediately and perform a caesarean section procedure.

CASE 3: A young man, upon consultation was advised by a Lasik eye clinic that his case was appropriate for a Lasik procedure and he would be able to enjoy life again without the use of glasses or contact lenses. After the procedure was performed, he was left with significant loss of sight and required cornea transplants.

SECTION 2

THE MEDICAL
MALPRACTICE
INSURANCE POLICY

The Money Insurance Policy

Almost all businesses handle money in some form or another be it while in transit or in cash counters or in a safe, all of which often present unwanted possibilities for business owners.

Businesses need to face the possibility of robbery on their premises realistically, thefts could take place when premises are trading or when closed and thieves could use stealth or bravado. Owners should ensure effective control and security measures are in place to avoid the financial and emotional after effects of being a victim.

Cash is very vulnerable when it is being moved even if armored vehicles or heavily armed police escorts are used.

Likewise, safes, given enough time and the right tools, any safe in the world can be broken into and in many cases it's often easier to just take the whole safe than to break into it inside the premises.

SECTION 2

THE MONEY INSURANCE POLICY

Who is the policy suitable for?

This policy is essential for businesses of any size and occupation if staff are occasionally or constantly handling or keeping money belonging to the business and when transiting money between different locations (for instance between a shop and the bank).

The policy is designed to cover loss of cash notes and coins, bank drafts, treasury notes, cheques, postal orders and current postage stamps. Other types can be also included such as credit card sales vouchers, instant lottery tickets, bus or transport tickets and telephone credit cards.

Cover description

The money insurance policy primarily provides cover against the following:

1. **Loss of money** as a result of robbery, burglary or hold-up whilst kept in a locked Safe, in locked counters, drawers, cash Registers, tills, cabinets during or outside business hours on the business premises.

2. **Loss of cash** while being transited in vehicles or on foot between specified locations on direct trips by authorized employees or messengers.

3. **Loss or damage** caused by thieves to safes, strong rooms and cases specifically designed for carrying money

What does it pay for?

Policy protection provides payment for the amount of any loss of money belonging to the Insured or for which the Insured is responsible and compensation for of loss of or damage to any safe, strong room or carrying case used for carrying money.

Possible policy extensions

At the request of the Insured, the policy can be extended at additional premium charges to include the risk of infidelity of the employees, personal accident following assault on employees, terrorism and disbursement risks.

The policy can be also extended to insure bullion in the form of ingots, bars, coins, jewelry, cash in ATM and cybercrime.

General exclusions

A clear cut list of exclusions applies. Shortage due to error or omission, losses due to the fraud or dishonesty of the employees of the Insured, unexplained losses and mysterious disappearances, loss or damage arising out of use of key to safe or strong room unless such keys are obtained by force or threat, money entrusted to any person other than the Insured or an authorized employee, legal liability, consequential loss, theft from an unsecured or unattended vehicle and consequential loss are excluded risks.

It is not common to find an excess applied to the claims admissible under the policy but it can be applied by the insurer if the nature of the risk warrants it.

Setting the sum insured

The sum insured needs to be specified for two activities as specified in the policy coverage:

1. The sum insured for a single carrying and the corresponding estimated annual amount of money in transit

2. The total sum insured for the maximum amount of money held in each safe and in counters or tills

3. The insured value for each safe or strong room, if loss or damage to safes is included in cover

Policy premium calculation

The premiums are based on the nature of the business, location and the security controls in place.

First, a premium rate per one thousand dollar (per mille) will be multiplied by the estimated annual money in transit to arrive at the annual premium for money in transit.

Then, a different premium rate per one hundred dollar (percent) is multiplied by the estimated total amount of money held in safes to arrive at the annual premium for money held in safes.

The total annual premium for the policy is the sum of both premiums calculated as described above.

What information do the insurers need to be told in an insurance application?

Largely a simple proposal form containing questions relating to past accident experience, building type of construction, type of business occupying the premises, business hours, specifications of safe or strong room, method and security aspects employed whilst money is transported and systems and procedures for protection of premises during and after office hours.

A COMMON MISCONCEPTION

Safes provide protection against all eventualities of risk!

History begs to differ on this one! It's important to know is that there are two general categories of safes: burglar safes and fire safes.

The specifications that are needed to provide protection against a forced entry are not necessarily the same as those that are needed to resist fire damage therefore safes are usually designed to provide better protection against one or the other, but not both.

Some fire safes will provide limited protection against burglary while some burglar safes will provide a limited degree of resistance against fire, a specialized safe of one type or the other is generally needed to provide the best protection against either fire or burglary.

Recent research findings and developing trends relating to theft and crime!

Sigmund Freud had recognized that humans have basic unconscious biological urges and desires such as the urge for food and sex. If people could not acquire them legally they would try to do so illegally.

Our parents teach us in our early childhood the moral values and rights and wrongs despite our instinctive nature to acquire what we desire, coaching us to have control over natural urges to acquire whatever is needed.

US research conducted in 2012, revealed that a third of burglars were involved in at least one business burglary and that at least two thirds of burglars did not gather information on their targets before committing the burglary, indicating that most burglaries were impulsive in nature. It was also revealed that 79% of burglars were interested in acquiring cash followed by jewelry at 68% and electronics at 56%.

Case Studies

The following claims scenarios highlight the range of potential accidents that could arise in the normal course of business.

CASE 1: Large amount of cash was stolen from an armored car while it was being transited from a major department store to a bank. The robbery occurred when two men posing as the employees of a well-known courier accompanied by two armed fake police officers walked into the department store and picked up half a million US dollars. They used a van branded in the corporate colors of the courier complete with its logo and an escort saloon car. The courier vehicle was later found dumped.

CASE 2: Thieves broke into a gym and stole a safe containing cash. The gym located on major high street was broken into at about 5:30am. After searching the building, the thieves broke into a cabinet and stole a safe which had USD 3,000 in cash inside it. They also broke the lock on a second safe, but that was empty.

CASE 3: Six thieves used distraction and deception to steal from a small motel. The owner said a man and a woman asked to see a room. Once they were out of the office, another man and three more women sneaked into the office, including one holding a baby. They stole a bag of cash and a small safe. Police learned the group used a similar tactic to target other motels in the area.

SECTION 2

THE MONEY
INSURANCE POLICY

33

The Group Personal Accident Insurance Policy

Few would differ that the key assets of any company are its employees, although when it comes down to considering insurance protection, buildings, contents, business interruption, vehicles and legal liability requirements usually take priority.

Workers have a right to a safe workplace and the law in most countries requires employers to provide their employees with safe and healthy workplaces.

If an employee is injured or is killed from an accident while on duty, the results can be devastating. Aside from the physical and emotional injury, the employee or his family may also come under immense financial strain because of the accident and the business could incur the costs associated with that event.

SECTION 2

THE GROUP PERSONAL ACCIDENT INSURANCE POLICY

Providing this cover to the employees invariably portrays a caring employer and can assist in the recruitment and retention of staff noting that the cost to business of such benefit is usually less than 1% of the salary roll.

Who is the policy suitable for?

The policy can be had by businesses and organizations of all sizes, ranging from multi-nationals to SMEs, through to non-commercial organizations such as charities, trade unions and social clubs.

Industries or business environments that present a greater chance of an on the job accident for instance in cases where they operate heavy machinery or drive long distances daily are ideal customers for this policy.

Workers in some industries such as transportation, manufacturing, construction and couriering have a greater chance of an on the job accident if they operate heavy machinery or drive long distances daily can benefit from such cover.

Cover description

Most commonly group personal insurance cover is provided for group schemes of at least 3 employees, entry age is 16 years up to a maximum age of 65 years and insures against injury, disability or death caused solely by violent, accidental, external and visible event. Twenty four hour anywhere in the world cover is the norm for policy coverage. Benefits would normally include:

- **Death** due to accident
    - » Compensation is equal to the sum insured.

- **Permanent Total Disability** due to accident (PTD), for example, loss of sight in both eyes, physical separation of two entire hands or entire feet or paralysis.

    » Compensation is equal to the sum insured.

- **Permanent Partial Disability** due to accident (PPD), for example, loss of toe or finger.

    » Compensation will be a certain proportion of the sum insured as determined by the policy conditions.

- **Temporary Total Disability** due to accident (TTD), for example, the inability to return to work for a number days, weeks or months.

- **Medical Expenses**
  Reimbursement for medical expenses incurred as a result of an accident subject to a maximum limit

What does it pay for?

In the event of an accidental death or permanent disability, insurers make a lump sum pay out to the Insured or his designated beneficiary. Medical expenses corresponding to an injury are reimbursable subject to a pre-agreed limit.

The Insured will receive weekly benefit payments for a pre-determined period (ranges from one to two years) in the event of temporary disability.

Possible policy extensions

Personal accident insurance policies can be extended to provide additional benefits for partial temporary disability due to accident, emergency medical evacuation, transportation of mortal remains and funeral expenses, accidental food poisoning, ambulance charges, home and vehicle modification expenses, residence/work expenses for driver or taxi to convey the injured employee and cover for temporary personnel replacement expenses to replace an employee.

Insurers may also waive the requirement for cover to be on named basis making the policy easier to administer for large employers or those with large seasonal variation in staffing.

Some insurers market special policies where they are willing to offer intensive coverage level by including some of or all of the following risks:

- high risk trades
- disturbed territories
- nuclear, chemical and biological attacks resulting from terrorism
- war, sabotage, terrorism

Adding additional benefits and special perils to the policy will entail additional premium charges.

General exclusions

The list of exclusions applicable is rather standardized. Existing disability prior to the inception of the policy and claims under more than one of the categories mentioned in the policy which exceed the sum insured are excluded by the policy.

Claims caused as a result of events such as intentional self-injury, suicide or attempted suicide, whilst under the influence of alcohol or drugs, whilst engaging in any sort or form of adventurous sport, committing any breach of law with criminal intent, child birth or pregnancy or related ailments, trespassing into any public or private property are commonly excluded.

Group personal accident policies rarely include an excess or a deductible.

Setting the sum insured

It is very difficult to put a financial value to a human life or to the loss of a vital limb or organ. Hence the principle of indemnity cannot be applied to personal accident policies.

The Insured is normally free to set the amount of the sum insured as long as it is commensurate with the age, occupation and position of each employee. Generally, it is fixed as a multiple of the annual income earned by the employee from gainful employment.

Policy premium calculation

Premiums are determined on the basis of the sum insured selected, age of the Insured, nature of work, salary levels and the optional benefit selected.

Generally, different rates will apply for different occupations and for different benefits, insurers generally categorize occupations in to 3 or 4 different categories dependent on the perceived risks an occupation may exhibit. For instance, category 1 may include clerical, administrative or other similar non-hazardous occupations, category 2, supervisors of manual workers and totally administrative job in industrial environments and category 3, would be high risk occupations involving heavy manual work.

A premium rate per one thousand dollar of the sum insured will be multiplied by the total sums insured to calculate the annual policy premium.

What information do the insurers need to be told in an insurance application?

The information required for a group personal accident quotation is very basic and is limited to information concerning number of employees, age of each employee, occupation, the sum insured required per employee, scope of cover and details of past claims experience.

A COMMON MISCONCEPTION

We have an Employers Liability policy, so there is no need for Personal Accident Insurance?

Employers Liability covers situations when there is an alleged negligence on behalf of the employer. Court judgment and eventual settlement of such cases may take months or even years to finalize.

Personal Accident cover in contrast, is none negligent and can extend to 24 hours anywhere in the world cover where the majority of incidents will arise. Payment under a Personal Accident policy is far quicker than a settlement under an Employers Liability policy and the money can be used almost immediately preventing the employee from pursuing an Employers Liability claim thus protecting the interests of the Employer in saving future premiums under Employer Liability policy.

Recent research findings and developing trends on accidental injuries

Research released in 2016 and conducted in the USA revealed that the number one cause of accidents at work is overexertion in carrying, pulling and lifting duties accounting for approximately USD15.1 billion in benefit costs in the USA. Slipping on wet floors and tripping over uneven or foreign objects was ranked in second place while falling from heights such as ladders or roofs ranked third.

Both employers and employees have a duty to minimize the risks as much as possible. Employers are legally bound to carry out a full risk assessment of possible accidents that might occur in and out of the workplace and to incorporate preventative measures in their health and safety procedures.

Employees likewise have a duty to understand and apply their company's health and safety procedures and to pay due care and attention to their own actions in the workplace to minimize the potential of accidents.

In contrast, every year more than 18,000 Americans die from accidental injuries that take place in the house, making homes the second most common accident location behind only cars on the road of such fatalities.

Away from the work environment and in studying accidents at the home, it appears that the most common cause of fatality at home is falls and slips claiming the lives of 6000 people per year, examples include falling in showers and slipping bathtubs. Poisoning is ranked in second place taking away nearly 5000 lives. People would be surprised to learn that taking medicine or inadvertently mixing different medicines is the leading cause of poisoning. Home

SECTION 2

THE GROUP PERSONAL ACCIDENT INSURANCE POLICY

fires and burns claim more than 3,000 lives annually and come in third place.

Clearly homeowners as well need to consider any significant safety risks and to take necessary steps to reduce these risks.

Case Studies

The following claims scenarios highlight the range of potential accidents that could arise in the normal course of business.

CASE 1: a sales manager while on a motor cycling holiday gets accidently killed in a motor traffic accident

CASE 2: while a factory worker is using a sheet metal cutting machine he accidently gets his fingers amputated

CASE 3: a lawyer losses sight in one eye as a result of an electric shock when he accidentally waters a Christmas tree with its lights on

The Property All Risks Insurance Policy

(Open Perils Property policy)

This policy provides a wider form of cover than that provided by the Fire insurance policy, in that the exclusions and limitations are key to determining what coverage is provided by this policy, it is recommended that the Fire insurance section presented in this book is read before proceeding here.

Even though an all-risk policy will cost more, in a world where freak accidents happen, the broader the insurance coverage the better off the Insured will be.

Who is the policy suitable for?

Most lenders require that an Insured carries an all risks policy to protect its investment. But it is of equal importance to leaseholders or tenants of residential and commercial property.

SECTION 2

THE PROPERTY ALL RISKS INSURANCE POLICY

All real and personal property can be included for insurance and may include all movable and immovable property such as buildings, plant and machinery, furniture, fixtures, fittings, office equipment, property held in trust or on commission, stocks and stock in progress, stocks at suppliers or customer's premises, machinery temporarily removed from the premises for repairs and other contents.

Cover description

The Property All Risks insurance policy covers loss arising from any fortuitous cause except those that are specifically excluded in the policy. The insurer must prove that the peril causing the damage is not excluded, otherwise, coverage applies.

The most common wording in use of a Property All Risks policy is what is referred to as the "London Market 7 or LM7" wording.

Example causes and resulting loss or damage include, fire, explosion of boilers, smoke, lightning, impact by vehicles, fallen trees, fallen cranes, burglary by forcible entry, burglary by hold-up, water damage due to bursting or overflowing of pipes and water tanks, rain damage, damage to electrical apparatus, electrical fluctuation, removal of debris, expert and architect fees, loss of rent, liability towards neighbors and liability towards co-owners.

What does it pay for?

The policy indemnifies the Insured for the direct costs associated with the replacement, rebuild or repair of buildings and contents caused by a peril not specifically excluded by the policy. The basis for compensation depends on whether the policy wording stipulates the use of the Replacement Value or Actual Cash Value calculation.

Possible policy extensions

The PAR policy wording is quite comprehensive in its scope, however the most significant extensions regularly asked for include sabotage and terrorism, business interruption, contingent business interruption, machinery breakdown and deterioration of stock.

Adding additional perils to the policy cover will entail additional premium charges.

General exclusions

The policy will exclude coverage for loss or damage resulting from war and war like operations, radioactive contamination or nuclear perils, pollution or contamination, electrical or mechanical breakdown, governmental seizure of property, spontaneous combustion, dishonesty or theft or unexplained or mysterious disappearance or inherent vice, consequential loss, deterioration of property due to change in temperature or humidity or failure or inadequate operation of an air conditioning cooling or heating system.

More often than not, the policy will exclude a certain monetary amount which the Insured shall bear.

Setting the sum insured

The same methods used for setting the sum insured of Fire insurance policies apply also to property all risks policies. The *Reinstatement Value* method and The *Market Value* method are the two most commonly used methods for this purpose (refer to the Fire insurance policy section).

Policy premium calculation

SECTION 2

THE PROPERTY ALL RISKS INSURANCE POLICY

The premium rate is largely determined by the location of the premises (for example, being located in flood or earthquake prone areas is considered high risk), the type of materials the building is constructed of, its overall condition and age (buildings made of brick will cost less to insure than those made out of timber), internal features such as separations or sectioning, the type of occupancy and the use of flammable or toxic chemicals or hazardous processes.

The insurers may allow some premium discount if the Insured applies stringent safety, security, accident prevention and protection measures (for example, fire sprinklers, substantial water storage or source, standby electricity generators etc.) in synch with good risk management and business continuity plans.

A premium rate per one thousand dollar will be multiplied by the sum insured deduced by any of the methods mentioned before to arrive at the annual policy premium.

What information do the insurers need to be told in an insurance application?

The most basic information requirement will include that concerning past accidents and claims experience, age and size of premises, building type of construction, type of business occupying the premises, fire detection, warning and fighting system, itemized list of the properties and contents to be covered. The level of detail required depends largely on the value of the property, occupation, the nature of content and the past accident history.

The Insured has to provide the breakdown of the values to be insured and state whether the cover will be on Reinstatement or Actual Value basis.

Additionally, the insurers may want to survey the premises to gather additional information and if the risk is deemed acceptable for insurance, the Insured may well receive a copy of the survey report containing a list of improvements to be made subject to a certain timeframe. A risk survey allows insurers to make well-informed decisions on the scope of the coverage and to avoid properties of a quality below its preferred threshold.

A COMMON MISCONCEPTION

If a sprinkler system is installed, it will cause more damage than the fire!

Contrary to popular belief, water damage from a sprinkler system will be much less severe than the damage caused by water from firefighting hose lines or smoke or heat damage if the fire goes unabated. Not only that, but sprinkler heads are normally individually activated by fire.

Recent research findings and developing trends relating to property losses

It's been reported that 80% of the world's largest cities are at risk of severe damage from earthquakes, while 60% are in danger from storm surges and tsunamis. There is increasing scientific evidence that impacts of climate change could cause sea levels to rise and could bring more frequent and more severe natural disasters, such as hurricanes, typhoons and extreme rainstorms.

The earthquakes which struck Tohoku, Japan in 2011 (an earthquake and tsunami) and Northbridge, USA in 1994 marked the latest largest losses in the development of growing losses from earthquakes over the twenty years and is mainly due to the ever increasing concentration of values and population in many earthquake prone major cities. In contrast, people have a general tendency to be less frightened of floods than of other natural events. Unlike earthquakes, people think that when it happens, they will be able to barricade themselves in or escape unharmed with their belongings. But experience has proved that floods can neither be entirely prevented, nor can they be completely controlled.

Manmade disasters can't be ignored either. There are plenty of events that could be cause for a catastrophe. Poor building product compliance has been a major issue around the globe, with rough estimates showing that the market penetration of non-conforming products is huge. Exterior cladding materials, for example, on modern towers are posing significant risk of fire. Cladding came into vogue over a decade ago and developers use it because it offers a beautiful external finish to buildings and is relatively simple and cheap to install. These buildings pose the risk of high-rise fires which can be extremely difficult to put out.

As already outlined there are many factors re compounding the rising cost of property claims with the trend towards ever higher values and risks that are increasingly interconnected and concentrated in areas with compound exposure.

Case Studies

The following claims scenarios highlight the range of potential accidents that could arise in the normal course of business.

CASE 1: After unusually heavy rainfall, the street across from the Insured's restaurant was flooded and some water was seeping through the front entrance. Also rain water was quickly accumulating on the building's flat roof but it wasn't draining off quickly enough, as a result water was seeping through the ceiling as well. The restaurant was badly damaged and the owner was forced to close the business until repairs to building and contents were completed.

CASE 2: More than 15 buildings in a downtown location sustained storm damage one early morning due to 100 miles per hour winds. Fire fighters from multiple fire districts responded to the scene. Damage to the buildings was extensive, torn down roofs and signboards, shattered window panes, heavy debris strewn everywhere, even nearby power lines were knocked down as a result of the storm.

CASE 3: In an area surrounded by offices, hotels and restaurants, a man died in an early morning attempted suicide when his light aircraft crashed into two buildings. The small plane clipped an office block and then slammed into a hotel building. The aircraft didn't explode however the cost of damage reparation to both of the high rise glass-clad buildings was extensive.

SECTION 2

THE PROPERTY ALL
RISKS INSURANCE
POLICY

35

The Professional Indemnity Insurance Policy

(Errors and Omissions insurance)

Professionals are expected to possess extensive technical knowledge in their specific area of expertise and are also required to perform their services as per certain standards of conduct, the use of which allows these professionals to enjoy a rewarding and lucrative career.

However, they may face a range of risks that are part of offering their services, such risks may include a client or group of clients filing a claim for damages because of a problem in the services the firm has offered.

Clients are more likely to resort to litigation when standards of conduct have not been met. The potential consequences of these suits or claims is serious, at the very least the business could incur legal costs to defend the claim in addition to liability to pay compensation as well as the claimant's costs and expenses.

SECTION 2

THE PROFESSIONAL INDEMNITY INSURANCE POLICY

Litigation can ultimately diminish a company's value, drive down sales or even cause a business to fold.

Who is the policy suitable for?

Professional indemnity insurance applies to individuals and organizations involved in providing consultancy, advice, opinion, design and analysis based extensively on personal knowledge and skills.

Typically recommended for accountants, IT consultants, financial advisors, journalists, engineers, solicitors, architects, interior decorators and others that provide advice, support or contractual work.

Cover description

Professional indemnity insurance protects the Insured against claims for alleged negligence or breach of duty arising from an act, error or omission in the performance of professional services.

Example causes of claims include:

- Professional negligence (i.e. making a mistake)
- Misleading or deceptive conduct
- Loss of client documents or data
- Loss of goods or money for which the business is responsible
- Unintentional breach of copyright or confidentiality
- Defamation and libel

Only civil liability claims are covered. Any liability arising out of any criminal act or act committed in violation of any law or ordinance is not usually covered.

What does it pay for?

Professional indemnity insurance provides protection against the legal costs and expenses incurred in defending a claim against the Insured as well as compensation payable to his client to rectify a mistake.

Professional indemnity policies can provide protection for settlements, judgments, investigation costs and defence costs.

Possible policy extensions

At the request of the Insured, the policy can be extended to include cover against dishonesty of employees, court attendance costs, extended reporting period beyond the policy expiry date, joint ventures and previous firms or previous partners.

Extending the policy cover in this way will entail additional premium charges.

General exclusions

Typically, policies will exclude losses resulting from employers liability, bodily injury and property damage (except where caused by a breach of professional duty), product liability, contractual liability, insolvency or bankruptcy of the Insured, intentional acts, fines and penalties, patents or trade secrets, claims by financially associated parties, war, terrorism, seepage and pollution.

A deductible for each and every loss may be applicable under the policy.

SECTION 2

THE PROFESSIONAL INDEMNITY INSURANCE POLICY

Setting the limit of indemnity

In a professional indemnity policy, the sum insured is referred to as the limit of indemnity. This limit is fixed per each accident with an additional aggregate limit per policy period.

The Insured must consider a worst case scenario if a mistake is made in work for a client and estimate the cost of putting it right. The Insured must also take into consideration claims inflation, third party legal fees, regulatory requirements and losses that could be incurred by the client as a result of the error.

Policy premium calculation

If the Insured is able to demonstrate high professional competence and show the insurers that it's doing a good job to prevent claims from arising wherever possible, then there would be reasonable expectations for reductions in the premium quoted.

Such as examples would be by ensuring employees have relevant experience and qualifications, business is structured properly, risk management and quality management systems are utilized and using signed terms and conditions with every contract.

The industry the business works in, the advice it gives, the service it offers and the size of the contracts it signs up are primary factors used by the insurers for setting the premium rates.

In most cases, the Insured's gross fee income for the last full financial year is used to forecast its base premium for the following year.

What information do the insurers need to be told in an insurance application?

This is one of those policies were a fully completed insurance proposal form is mandatory given the extensive level of information required.

about the ownership, the directors and the executive team and their CVs, number of staff, the professional services offered activities, gross fees or turnover payable by clients, gross fees paid to sub-contractors, extent of work carried out internationally, desired limit of indemnity, past accidents, risk management practices and claims experience.

A COMMON MISCONCEPTION

Our firm only handles small assignments, therefore there is no need to purchase a large limit of indemnity!

Unfortunately, small and newly established businesses tend to believe that there is a strong correlation between fee income from an assignment and professional negligence exposure.

This is a dangerous misconception, since large claims, defence and legal representation costs have arisen from assignments or projects that generated only minimal fee income.

Recent research findings and developing trends relating to losses effecting professional advisors

Research conducted in the United Kingdom in 2015 revealed that small and medium-sized enterprises

SECTION 2

THE PROFESSIONAL INDEMNITY INSURANCE POLICY

(SMEs) in the legal profession are the most likely to have professional indemnity, with 88 per cent of businesses taking out insurance. This is followed by financial services which would include insurance brokers at 59 per cent and scientific, technical and engineering research at 52 per cent.

In a UK survey, again conducted in 2015, it was determined that more than 320,000 small and micro businesses had lost an average of over GBP20,000 in the past 12 months due to poor professional advice or service. IT consultants were named the most often in the survey for giving bad advice with 44 per cent of businesses affected by poor guidance.

Case Studies

The following claims scenarios highlight the range of potential accidents that could arise in the normal course of business.

CASE 1: A stock broking firm was sued by its client when it was alleged that the investment advice it had given breached its duty of care because it was incorrect. The client had purchased stock in reliance upon that advice incurring as a result a financial loss.

CASE 2: A graphic designer working on a website project for an online furniture store had used pictures on the website for which a fee was not paid to the copyright owner. The online store owners were sued by the pictures owner. The store owner in turn sued the website designer for reimbursement and compensation.

CASE 3: An event organizer responsible for booking a conference hall for a business celebrating its 50th anniversary forgot to confirm the booking. As a result, the conference hall was not available to their client and the event had to be postponed for another 45 days. The event organizer was sued for the cancellation fees that their client had to pay to speakers and caterers as well as the cost of printed literature that could not be reused.

SECTION 2

THE PROFESSIONAL
INDEMNITY
INSURANCE POLICY

The Products Liability Insurance Policy

(Products-Completed Operations Insurance)

Consumers expect seller's involvement at just about every stage of the lifecycle of a product, but however well-designed the product that is manufactured or sold might be, accidents do happen and it's vital that proper protection is purchased. In today's litigious society, it is not even necessary for the business to be the manufacturer of the product because sellers are often sued alongside the manufacturers.

Since virtually every new product carries some unknown risk, a possibility always exists that the product may cause injuries. Defective or dangerous products are the cause of thousands of injuries every year.

Thousands of product injury lawsuits are filed each year, as the number of claims has risen, so too has the number of businesses forced to file bankruptcy because of costly suits.

SECTION 2

THE PRODUCTS LIABILITY INSURANCE POLICY

An increasing number of businesses are claiming that they have taken products off the market and stopped research on some products for fear of liability, product injuries now represent a major cost of introducing new products into a market.

Consumer protection groups, on the other hand, claim that the potential threat of product liability suits forces manufacturers and distributors to make product safety a priority and that those that suffer injuries should be compensated for their injuries.

Some economies have also suffered from the rise in product liability claims. When companies facing massive lawsuits have been forced to scale down their operations, one of the results is an inevitable loss of jobs.

Who is the policy suitable for?

A business should consider product liability insurance if it designs, manufactures or constructs or erects, supplies or sells or services or gives away for free a physical product. This would include designers, manufacturers, distributors, wholesalers, importers and retailers involved throughout the chain of trade.

It is important to clarify this further, product liability should be bought if the Insured is a:

- manufacturer or retailer that supplies its own brand of products
- business that repairs, alters or services an existing product
- business that recycles or repurposes or rebrands an existing product
- Importer of products from places where the safety requirements differ from the country it is sold in

The Insured might be liable if the business name is on the product and will remain liable even if the manufacturer has gone out of business.

In most cases, some form of product liability coverage will be present in a standard commercial general liability policy. However covering this topic separately is intended to reinforce the growing importance of this policy.

Cover description

Cover is afforded to the Insured against financial loss for claims resulting from defective design, defective manufacture or defective marketing (failure to warn or inadequate user instructions) causing:

- accidental death or bodily injury or
- accidental damage to property belonging to a third party

Most products liability insurance is offered on claims-occurring basis rather than on a claims-made basis, however, for certain industries such as pharmaceutical and food supplements manufacturers, insurers may insist that the policy be on claims-made basis.

What does it pay for?

Typically, the policy protects against awards for pain and suffering to anyone that is injured and their associated medical expenses, compensation to those that suffered lost wages, physical loss or damage caused to goods or land or buildings or fixtures belonging to others, court awarded damages, legal defence fees and punitive damages.

Possible policy extensions

SECTION 2

THE PRODUCTS
LIABILITY INSURANCE
POLICY

The most common extensions offered include product recall expenses, court attendance expenses and worldwide cover including USA and Canada.

Adding these additional covers will entail additional premium charges.

General exclusions

Typically the list of policy exclusions excludes all liability arising from replacing, reinstating, rectifying, recalling or guaranteeing product performance, products sold or supplied for use in a craft designed to travel through air or space.

It also excludes, liquidated damages or fines or penalties which attach solely because of a contract or agreement and liability arising out of professional advice given by the Insured for a fee.

Common standard exclusions such as ionizing radiation or contamination, asbestos, war (whether war be declared or not), civil war, invasion, act of foreign enemy, rebellion, revolution, insurrection or usurped power also appear in the policy.

Universally speaking, it is found that policies issued by non-north American insurers will exclude from cover suits brought against the Insured in USA and Canada as they are considered expensive litigious jurisdictions. However, the Insured may request that the policy is extended to cover North American jurisdictions at an additional premium.

Setting the liability limit

The Insured should make an assessment of the limits required based on the type of products they supply and their potential exposure to loss.

The limit of indemnity is fixed per any one occurrence and usually there is a ceiling on the number of occurrences payable during the policy period and is referred to as the general annual aggregate.

The per occurrence Limit is the most an insurer will pay for the sum of damages for bodily injury and property damage arising out of any one occurrence. Any such sums paid will reduce the amount of the applicable aggregate limit available for any other payment. Though, some policies may be issued without an annual aggregate.

Policy premium calculation

The insurer may adjust the resulting premium to reflect positive features implemented by the Insured such as product labels being plain to see in how to use and how not to use the product, performing quality assurance control checks before selling the product, making sure that the product works as stated and that it is free of product defects and having good risk management practices will also help greatly.

The sales volume or turnover of the business is used as the basis for calculating the premium. A premium rate per one thousand dollar will be multiplied by the estimated total turnover to arrive at the annual policy premium. The premium rates on such policies are decided based upon the type of product, volume of sales, and the role of the insured in the process.

SECTION 2

THE PRODUCTS
LIABILITY INSURANCE
POLICY

What information do the insurers need to be told in an insurance application?

Insurers require extensive information through a detailed proposal form which will focus on many factors of the products and business including nature and specification of products, volume of products distribution, what they are used for and who will be using them, how long they are intended to last and what they are made of.

Further questions will relate to how clearly defined are the usage instructions, directions and guarantees or warrantees that are provided with the product and what claims the manufacturer or distributor make about the product, either in writing or in demonstration in the media. Past claims experience is also required.

A COMMON MISCONCEPTION

A product has to be defective or faulty for a product liability claim to arise!

No. This is a very common misconception of the nature of the cover. The use of the words *defective* and *faulty* is widespread in many authoritative definitions and articles including ones from organizations and businesses that really should know better! The fact that the product was the cause of loss or damage to a third party is sufficient reason for filing a claim regardless if it was defective or not.

Recent research findings and developing trends on products liability

Statistics by the US District Courts show that approximately 43,000 products liability cases were filed during the 12 months period ending March 31, 2015. Jury Verdict Research study determined the median jury verdict in product liability cases at USD1.5m for the 2000 to 2006 period, and 30% of the cases resulted in verdicts over USD1m. Court awards for product liability cases ranked second after medical malpractice and far exceeded those granted in all other types of cases.

The US' Consumer Product Safety Commission (CPSC), in 2015, imposed more than USD26.4 million in fines for corporate violations of product safety standards (10 cases) compared to USD5.2 million (4 cases) in 2014 and USD7.9 million (7 cases) in 2013. As can be deduced from these figures, the average penalty imposed by the agency more than doubled from USD 1.1 million in 2013 to more than USD2.6 million in 2015. As of writing this book, until the middle of 2016, there were 2 cases to date with fines totaling an amazing USD17.5 million which average more than USD 8.5 million per case.

Moreover, products liability claims have trended to become more international in scope, complex and costly as better awareness of compensation and US style litigation continues to spread.

Recall cases from motor vehicle makers are becoming more frequent and more expensive, in 2015, a German motor vehicle manufacturer's alleged use of software to manipulate emissions test results and the subsequent recall of nearly 500,000 diesel-powered cars is estimated to cost the company in excess of USD 60 billion.

SECTION 2

THE PRODUCTS LIABILITY INSURANCE POLICY

Restaurants have also made the media headlines in a major way. A US casual restaurant chain of Mexican food has since October 2015 allegedly experienced three consecutive outbreaks involving three separate pathogens. At least 37 people have been sickened with E. coli. The chain has had to shut down more than 50 of its restaurants even though only 8 had drawn concerns. Class action suits are before US courts.

Case Studies

The following claims scenarios highlight the range of potential accidents that could arise in the normal course of business.

CASE 1: A lady filed a suit against a manufacturer of a copper intrauterine device she had worn under prescription by her doctor. A year and a half later after usage, she removed the device hoping to become pregnant only to find she had become infertile. Doctors attributed her sterility to a disease frequently associated with the use of this device. She filed a product liability suit against the manufacturer holding them liable for her infertility.

CASE 2: More than 400 people reported getting sick after allegedly eating a certain yogurt brand produced in the USA. The company had to advise consumers and retail stores to destroy all varieties of yogurt after reporting that it had been contaminated by a mold associated with dairy products. The company suffered from a significant financial loss as a result of the product destruction and disposal, the negative publicity and the cost of law suits brought against it by some customers.

CASE 3: A residential apartment in Dubai allegedly caught on fire after the owner plugged in their new hover-board (electric two wheel scooter) purchased online three days earlier. There were several other reported fires that had been linked to the hover-boards. Industry professionals deemed them unsafe due to a noncompliant plug for electrical outlets and other parts.

Despite hover-boards being one of the most popular toys of the 2015 holiday season, the online retailer fearing further accidents had to remove the product from its website and sent an email to all of its customers advising them to dispose of the product and stating that it has begun to process refunds.

SECTION 2

THE PRODUCTS
LIABILITY INSURANCE
POLICY

The Property Terrorism and Sabotage Insurance Policy

Acts of terrorism against business property have potentially far reaching political and economic effects. The bombing of the World Trade Centre in New York is estimated to have cost approximately USD 700 million in disrupted business in the first week alone. As politically motivated terrorism and sabotage incidents generate more media coverage, businesses, especially those owned by foreign companies will find themselves increasingly targeted.

Although many governments have introduced state funded terrorism insurance and reinsurance facilities that may be referred to as terrorism schemes, funds or pools (the Terrorism Risk Insurance Act (TRIA) in the U.S. which in 2015 became known as TRIPRA, Pool Re in the UK, SASRIA in South Africa and AWRIS in Bahrain), an extensive commercial terrorism insurance market still exists for terrorism events.

Unfortunately the potential problem with government schemes can be clearly demonstrated with the example of the Boston Marathon bombing in the U.S. which unlike the Oklahoma and 9/11 losses, was not officially designated as a terrorist attack by the US government. This meant there has been no payment to Insureds affected by the bombing under TRIA, the U.S. sponsored scheme. Similarly, attacks by anti-abortion, animal rights or other extremist groups would not necessarily fit the definition of a terrorist event by many of the government sponsored schemes.

Terrorism insurance policies, however, do not require an event to be confirmed by the government as an act of terrorism and would consider an attack caused by a wider range of incidents as a potentially covered loss.

Away from home, since no one can predict when or where new terrorist action may occur, the implications of civil unrest abroad and the level of world economic growth are difficult questions to answer. Companies trading, investing and manufacturing in developing countries may suffer as the political climate changes with little warning.

Risk levels are continually changing across the world, however, certain areas and in particular the Western economies are witnessing increased risk levels due to the increased terror threat presented by extremists.

Who is the policy suitable for?

The services and industrial sectors need to consider their level of exposure to this type of events, many companies feel exposed to the threat of terrorism activity because of the nature of the business or the territories in which they operate, some may appear readily exposed while others may not be so obvious, examples would include the following:

- Hotels and tourist resorts, stadiums, amusement parks and other leisure venues
- Communication and public transport, including telephone, airports, metros and railways
- Government buildings and foreign missions, including ministry and embassy properties
- Utilities, including power generation, water desalination, oil and gas installations
- Malls and shopping arcades
- Places of worship

Sometimes contractors may be required by their clients to carry terrorism insurance as a condition of the contract or a lender may also require coverage for their investments. Furthermore, businesses that are located where known acts of terrorism have occurred may also be required to carry terrorism insurance.

Cover description

In general and in their most basic form, Property Terrorism and Sabotage policies cover the business against loss or damage to the insured property resulting from fire and explosion caused by acts committed for political, religious, ideological or similar reasons.

There are varying definitions of sabotage and terrorism for insurance purposes so we are concerned with the most common definitions in order that the intention of what is to be covered by a typical policy is clear. The scope of cover will as a result, depend on the definitions used and the exclusions that apply.

Terrorism, is an act involving the use of force or violence, of any person or group of persons, whether acting alone

SECTION 2

THE PROPERTY TERRORISM AND SABOTAGE INSURANCE POLICY

or on behalf of or in connection with any organization, committed for political, religious or ideological purposes including the intention to influence any government or to put the public in fear for such purposes, that causes damage or destruction of property.

Sabotage, similarly, means the deliberate subversive act or series of acts committed for political, religious or ideological purposes including the intention to influence any government and to put the public in fear for such purposes and causes damage or destruction of property.

Mobile or fixed property, buildings owned or rented, stock-in-trade, machinery, furniture, fixtures and fittings, office equipment and all other property belonging to the insured business can be included under the policy.

It is important though not to confuse this policy with other broader form terrorism insurance policies, for instance, Political Violence insurance, protects against financial loss as the consequence of terrorism, insurrection, revolution, rebellion, civil unrest, malicious damage, politically motivated sabotage, strikes, riots and civil commotion, armed uprising, mutiny, coup d'état, war and civil war.

Political Risk insurance (also known as **Comprehensive Political Violence**) policies, on the other hand, provide coverage for, political violence, expropriation, currency inconvertibility, non-payment, and contract frustration risks.

What does it pay for?

The policy indemnifies the property owner for the direct costs associated with the replacement, rebuild or repair of buildings and contents insured caused by named perils.

Possible policy extensions

The insurers may be willing to extend the policy to include cover for strikes, riots, civil commotion, malicious damage, insurrection, revolution, rebellion, mutiny, coup d'etat and war. Few specialist insurers may also provide for nuclear, chemical, biological and radiological extensions but would be limited in scope and command high prices.

The policy may be also extended to include business interruption, contingent business interruption, prevention or restriction of access to premises and utilities, loss of income including rental income following property damage by an insured peril, terrorism liability from a terrorist attack for damages to third parties or employees who are injured.

It is important to define some of the perils mentioned above:

Insurrection, means the violent rising of citizens or subjects in resistance to their government.

Rebellion consists of organized and open resistance by force and arms to the laws or operation of government, committed by its citizens, while, *Mutiny,* is defined as the willful resistance by members of legally constituted, armed or peacekeeping forces acting in concert against a superior officer.

Coup d'état, is the overthrow of an existing government by a group of its citizens or subjects.

Extending the policy coverage by adding additional perils will entail additional premium charges.

General exclusions

Many of the terrorism policies available include exclusions relating to the following risks:

- burglary, housebreaking, theft or larceny
- confiscation, requisition, detention, legal or illegal occupation of property, war, invasion, act of foreign enemy, hostilities or warlike operations (whether war be declared or not), civil war, or seizure of power arising from a military conspiracy
- nuclear detonation, nuclear reaction, nuclear radiation or radioactive contamination, chemical or biological release or exposure
- attacks by electronic means (cyber) including computer hacking or the introduction of any form of computer virus

A percentile deductible is usually applicable which would be subject to a minimum fixed amount. For example, 10% of claim amount subject to a minimum of USD 10,000 for each and every claim.

Setting the sum insured

Typically for Terrorism and Sabotage insurance policies, the sum insured is based on a "Loss Limit" and not the full value of the property to be insured and is obviously agreed with the Insured in advance.

On some occasions, the insurers may be willing to insure the full value but this becomes more difficult if the value of the property is huge, also the location and the occupancy play a big role here.

Policy premium calculation

Geographical and political considerations greatly influence the pricing of terrorism policies. The pricing of terrorism risks has traditionally been influenced by the country security rating making severe and frequent attacks a critical factor.

The premium is based on a tariff system developed by insurers which depends on the locations of the business and the type of use or occupancy of the property.

A premium rate per one hundred dollar of the sum insured will be multiplied by the total sum insured to arrive at the annual policy premium.

What information do the insurers need to be told in an insurance application?

Underwriting questions will relate to exact locations and addresses of business or branches or subsidiaries, proximity to landmark properties or potential terrorist target businesses, values per location, type of use or occupancy of the property, limits of indemnity required and claims history. Much of this information would have been provided anyway if this policy is accompanying a Fire policy.

Insurers treat the rating of this policy in the same way they rate natural catastrophe covers and a major concern would be the aggregated property value exposure of more than one insurance policy within the radius of a blast zone. For example, a bomb explosion on one street could damage multiple properties.

SECTION 2

THE PROPERTY TERRORISM AND SABOTAGE INSURANCE POLICY

A COMMON MISCONCEPTION

Terrorism is just another insurance risk as devastating as hurricanes and it can be insured in traditional ways!

Not quite true. Both could be considered to be unpredictable, but insurers have more than 100 years of reliable weather data to try to predict their hurricane exposure and businesses have a similar amount of experience with managing weather risks. That is hardly true with terrorism.

Terrorism is hardly a routine business risk, rather, it's an act of war waged on individuals and businesses by non-traditional combatants unhappy with the policies of government.

Recent research findings and developing trends on political violence

There is no doubt that political violence threats are increasing around the world due to various contributory factors including perceived political injustice, economic deprivation and freely available instant mass communication tools to name just a few. Social networking has played an important part in empowering those who previously had no voice in agitating dissatisfaction and unrest and has enabled disruptors to mobilize demonstrators.

It is estimated that the damage to infrastructure following the Arab spring in the Middle East reached USD 461 billion. Businesses have overwhelmingly been the favorite target of terrorists.

In 2014, the Institute for Economics and Peace (IEP) estimated the global economic fallout of acts of terror at USD 52.9 billion compared with 51.5 billion in the aftermath of September 11. This is a 61 per cent increase from the previous year and a ten-fold increase since 2000. In total, 93 countries experienced a terrorist incident in 2014, up from 88 in 2013.

According to a market survey of 17 industry segments published in 2015, education organizations had the highest take-up rate for terrorism insurance in 2014. Financial institutions, real estate, technology and telecommunications companies had the next highest take-up rates, all at or above 70%.

Since 2006, seventy per cent of all deaths from terrorism in the West were perpetrated by lone wolf terrorists. According to the IEP, Islamic fundamentalism was not the main cause of terrorism in the West over the last nine years. Eighty per cent of deaths by lone wolf terrorists in the West were driven by right wing extremism, nationalism, anti-government sentiment and political extremism and other forms of supremacy.

Case Studies

The following claims scenarios highlight the range of potential accidents that could arise in the normal course of business.

CASE 1: In Paris, on 13th November 2015, suicide bombers carried out a series of mass shootings and bombings at cafés, restaurants and a concert hall. Estimates put the death toll at 130 people and there were 368 people who were wounded. The French economy was estimated to have lost more than USD 2 billion in business due mainly to subdued tourism and consumer spending.

CASE 2: In 2010, political protests and demonstrations in Bangkok against the Thai government caused the death of nearly 100 people and more than USD1 billion in property damage and business interruption. In the event the second biggest shopping centre in south-east Asia at the time was destroyed.

CASE 3: An al-Qaeda group was behind suicide bombings at three American owned chain hotels in the centre of Amman, Jordan in 2005. The attacks rocked the Grand Hyatt Hotel, the Radisson SAS Hotel and Days Inn killing 60 people and injuring 115 others.

Useful reading

The Global Terrorism Database (GTD).

The Aon Terrorism and Political Risk Map, 2015. Launched by Aon Risk Solutions, in partnership with The Risk Advisory Group.

Terrorism Risk Assessment: Best Practices for Insurers and Reinsurers, 2055. AIR Worldwide Corporation

Country Reports on Terrorism 2014. US Department of State.

The Arab Spring Cost Report, 2015. The Arab Strategy Forum.

National Consortium for the Study of Terrorism and Responses to Terrorism: Annex of Statistical Information. U.S. Department of State.

The Trade Credit Insurance Policy

In conducting trade, protracted delays in payment, insolvent buyers, and political uncertainty are ever present exposures of trade.

Managing credit and counterparty risks has become one of the top risks facing distributors and manufacturers in doing international trade. Accounts receivable are very often the largest uninsured asset on a business' balance sheet even though it is also the primary source of revenue.

As many businesses look to enter new markets and extend their supply chains across several global regions the need to protect themselves from risks involving commercial trade debts increases.

If a buyer does not pay for the goods supplied or services rendered, the effects can be detrimental to the seller's balance sheet, bottom line and ultimately its future success. Moreover, unfamiliarity with new buyers may deter sellers from extending credit necessary to conduct domestic or international business.

SECTION 2

THE TRADE CREDIT INSURANCE POLICY

Businesses using trade credit insurance can enhance their bank financing in terms of improving the lending relationship, gain access to more capital at reduced rates, enhance their balance sheet, improve the quality of their bottom line and grow profitably. Equally importantly, is the ability it gives the supplier to offer longer credit terms to the buyer therefore enhancing the competitiveness of the supplier.

Who is the policy suitable for?

Trade credit insurance is a business-to-business tool that manufacturers, traders and services providers can make use of as a good alternative to other loss mitigation methods most commonly, letters of credit, factoring, cash-in-advance or self-insurance.

Coverage can be provided to companies with domestic or export sales, as well as to lenders that finance trade receivables.

Businesses using trade credit insurance can enhance their bank financing in terms of improving the lending relationship, gain access to more capital at reduced rates, enhance their balance sheet, improve the quality of their bottom line and grow profitably. Equally importantly, is the ability it gives the supplier to offer longer credit terms to the buyer therefore enhancing the competitiveness of the supplier.

This policy however is not suitable for retailers or suppliers that sell exclusively to governments.

Cover description

Trade credit insurance provides cover against the sudden and unexpected commercial risk beyond Insured's control that a buyer does not pay or that a buyer is overdue with a scheduled payment.

Non-payment due to buyer being declared bankrupt or under bankruptcy protection arrangements or becomes insolvent, or other similar legal status are usually covered under such policy.

Trade credit insurance policies can be flexible and allow the Insured to cover the entire portfolio or just specific key accounts against insolvency, bankruptcy and bad debts. Covering the whole portfolio is the most common type of cover and is normally referred to as Whole-Turnover cover.

Trade credit insurance is normally for short-term account receivables for instance for those due within 12 months.

What does it pay for?

The policy will pay out a percentage of the outstanding debt as a result of an admissible loss. This percentage usually ranges from 75% to 95% of the invoice amount.

The Insured will retain the balance of the loss in the form of coinsurance or a deductible.

Possible policy extensions

Since most of these policies are tailor-made to each business the issue of extensions is almost irrelevant here, however, one notable requirement might be that of insuring against the risk of non-payment due to political risks, one such example is the risk that money or payments

SECTION 2

THE TRADE CREDIT INSURANCE POLICY

cannot be transferred from one country to another due to civil unrest.

Political risks include war, strikes, riots, protests, or other civil unrest. With a trade credit insurance policy providing cover for political risks, not getting paid as a result of these occurrences would be covered.

Some insurers may be willing to offer more bespoke extensions, including:

- **Pre-delivery** and **work-in-progress**, provides safeguards against the Insured's financial loss due to a customer becoming insolvent before work is completed but after the Insured has incurred costs of material or labor. If a project for example fails, the Insured is not burdened with the debt.

- **Supplier default**, provides protection against financial losses resulting from a supplier going out of business. This includes the costs associated with finding new suppliers, the loss of advance payments made to the supplier and any possible fines or damages for late delivery.

Extensions to the standard policy coverage will entail additional premium charges.

General exclusions

Exclusions generally apply to goods sold on consignment, disputed debts between buyer and Insured, buyers that are subsidiary or associated companies of the Insured, products sold to insolvent buyers, buyers who are already overdue with payments to the Insured, losses resulting from dishonest or illegal acts, losses resulting from nuclear events or political risks or terrorism and shipments made when the Insured was insolvent.

Trade credit policies regularly include a deductible in the form of a waiting period which must elapse before any debt is payable, this is normally between 60 and 180 days.

Setting the sum insured or the credit limit

A discretionary amount is usually agreed with the Policyholder up to which they may trade under the cover of the policy without notifying the insurer. Any exposure exceeding this discretionary amount must be advised to the insurer and confirmed by means of a written credit limit.

The level of the limit is set at the maximum amount that can be owed by the buyer at any time.

In a Whole-Turnover trade credit insurance policy all buyers are covered. The entire buyer portfolio would be constantly monitored by the insurer and the Insured is advised about the status of every buyer.

Trade credit insurance policies are somewhat different from other types of insurance policies in that the insurer has the right to reduce or cancel a credit limit for a particular buyer at any time, usually as a result of negative information or bad experience with that buyer allowing the insurer to bring down the exposure immediately. In this way Insurers apply hands on approach to the policy throughout its duration.

For exports and international trade, the policy may well be subject to a country specific limit of liability in addition to a maximum policy limit.

Policy premium calculation

The insurer will be able to offer better prices when it is evident that trading terms are well defined and agreed between the business and its customers and that credit application forms are always completed by customers. Other important factors influencing the price include the trade sector a business trades in, size of its turnover, debt loss over the last few years, the credit worthiness of the larger debtors and the limits required.

Premium rates are generally calculated as a percentage of estimated business turnover. Since the future turnover is only an estimate at inception of policy, the exact premium wouldn't be known. Therefore, a minimum premium amount is usually an integral part of the policy. At expiry of the policy, the actual turnover is used to calculate the final premium amount due to the insurer.

An alternative annual premium calculation method would be to apply a premium rate percentage to the approved credit limits.

As mentioned earlier, a business can choose between insuring a single transaction or all its sales as a consequence this can influence the premium rate significantly.

What information do the insurers need to be told in an insurance application?

Given the complexity of these risks, insurers will require thorough understanding of the Insured's trade sector, financial health, funding requirements, internal credit management and collection procedures and risk and business strategies.

In addition to the above, insurers will usually require, a list of the Insured's top 10 to 20 buyers, list of buyers broken down by country (for exporters), details of the aged accounts receivables covering the previous 12 months of trading and three year's history of debtor delinquencies and credit losses.

A COMMON MISCONCEPTION

Credit Life insurance and Trade Credit insurance are different names for the same coverage!

In fact, they are totally different!

Credit life is purchased by an individual to protect against the risk of loss of income needed to repay debts. It is therefore, a life insurance policy designed to pay off a borrower's debt if that borrower dies.

Trade Credit insurance on the other hand, covers payment default risks resulting from trade with local and international buyers. It is purchased by a supplier as an alternative to demanding prepayment or letter of credit from their buyers.

Recent research findings and developing trends relating to international trade risks

During the 2007 to 2009 global financial collapse, many businesses found that their insurers withdrew trade credit insurance, as they couldn't continue insuring credit given to failing buyers both local and international resulting in a negative effect on sales growth as sellers were not able to extend the same trade credit facilities that they provided before. Alternative solutions available to business were more expensive financing products such as letters of credit or using their own funds to finance their trade.

Now consider the very recent easing of economic sanctions on Iran during 2016, which is widely expected to see as much as USD150 billion worth of Iranian assets unblocked and consequently will ignite the interests of

SECTION 2

THE TRADE CREDIT INSURANCE POLICY

foreign businesses from all over the globe. Exploring such trading opportunities with Iran would be enhanced with the availability of trade credit insurance.

Euro zone research spanning 29 countries conducted in 2015 has shown that 32% of companies surveyed see a clear connection between not being able to hire more and late payments. 24% of companies surveyed also indicated that late payments contribute to the need to lay off staff.

Looking at another survey this time from the UK. It was found that businesses in the higher turnover bands were more risk averse than the smaller businesses despite the fact that it is the smaller companies which suffer the greatest should a customer default. The smaller companies with turnover of USD1.5m to USD7.5m used advance payments rather than other risk methods.

Case Studies

The following claims scenarios highlight the range of potential accidents that could arise in the normal course of business.

CASE 1: A truck spare parts distributor had extended to an importer and for several years USD120,000 of credit for up to 90 days. The importer misses on two payments but the distributor continues deliveries, the importer eventually files for bankruptcy protection with debts to the distributor and other creditors, exceeding USD2.5m.

CASE 2: A European financial consultancy firm provided consultancy services on commodities price forecasting and forex trading strategies to a foreign private bank. The bank made fee payments promptly and there were never any issues until the president of the country was unexpectedly overthrown in a coup d'état. In the aftermath, all banks were nationalized and the consultants were not able to collect their last fee payment.

CASE 3: A clothing manufacturer sourcing fabrics and materials from local suppliers was only marginally profitable until 2006. The financial crisis which started in 2007 hurt company sales and the manufacturer had to file for bankruptcy protection. Creditors eventually collected 45% of the value of stock supplied to the now out of business manufacturer.

Useful reading

Overseas Business Risk. A collection of online information for UK businesses on how to identify and guard against security and political risks when trading overseas. From: Foreign & Commonwealth Office and UK Trade & Investment.

Testing the Trade Credit and Trade Link: Evidence from Data on Export Credit Insurance. World Trade Organization Economic Research and Statistics Division.

SECTION 2

THE TRADE CREDIT
INSURANCE POLICY

39

The Workmen Compensation Insurance Policy

A key part of running any business is keeping employees safe at work. If a worker does suffer from an injury, workers compensation policy can provide employees with the needed protection and compensation.

It's generally considered that the more skilled a workforce is, the less likely they are to have accidents at work. When an employee has an accident, the employer's response in most cases can determine whether or not that employee will return to the job again after recovering. If the employee feels disconnected during the recovery period, they will probably not return.

The workmen compensation policy is the primary method by which an employer can demonstrate the ability to satisfy labor employment obligations stipulated by the laws and regulations enacted in most countries. The insurance

SECTION 2

THE WORKMEN COMPENSATION INSURANCE POLICY

policy stands subject to the provisions of the prevailing workmen compensation acts or labor laws.

Who is the policy suitable for?

Almost every business no matter how many employees it has needs workers compensation insurance.

Contractors, volunteers, employees in private homes, farmhands, maritime employees, catering employees, casual workers, office and clerical staff and many others must be insured to protect the business from being sued by its employees for workplace related injury or illness or even death.

In most countries around the world, Workers Compensation insurance is a government mandated insurance program that employers are required to purchase to ensure medical bills and some lost wages are paid to employees injured or made ill on the job.

Cover description

The workers compensation policy generally provides insurance cover in the event of an employee while carrying out job related tasks is:

- Temporarily disabled due to injury or illness, can be partial or total

    » Temporary partial disability benefits, are payable when an employee is away from work beyond the specified excess period but is able to return to work in a limited capacity that would partially affect the employee's income.
    In contrast, temporary total disability benefits, are payable when an employee

is unable to be employed in any capacity for a period of time that exceeds the specified waiting period.

- Permanently disabled due to injury or illness, can be partial or total

  » Permanent partial disability payments, are payable when an employee who is no longer able to return to work with sufficient capacity to perform usual prior duties or if part or all of the function of a specific body part is lost due to a work related amputation or other disability.
  In contrast, permanent total disability payments, are payable to an employee who can no longer be employed in any capacity.

- Killed due to injury or illness

- Incurs medical expenses, for the initial treatment and subsequent treatments plus physical therapy or vocational rehabilitations

The policy would respond to claims regardless of who was at fault in the accident.

What does it pay for?

Although the compensation payable under the policy is usually modest, the policy provides the Insured with protection, based on the type and severity of illness or accident, against the costs of:

- weekly replacement income for lost wages while the employee is off from work, usually two thirds of the salary and up to a certain

SECTION 2

THE WORKMEN COMPENSATION INSURANCE POLICY

- statutory amount
- medical care expenses incurred in the treatment of the employee
- lump sum pay-out for any permanent injuries
- costs for retraining or skill enhancement after injury or illness if the employee is unable to recover completely and don't return to work for the same employer
- benefits to dependents of employee who is killed on the job

It is almost universally ruled that if a person collects workers compensation benefits, the employee cannot sue the employer.

Possible policy extensions

The policy cover can be extended subject to additional premium charges to include cover against employers liability, accidents occurring outside duty hours (24 hours cover) and compensation for burial expenses for employees killed on the job.

General exclusions

This policy will exclude any injury or disease sustained outside the agreed geographical area e.g. country or state, the Insured's liability to employees of contractors to the Insured, any accident directly attributed to Influence of alcohol or drugs, self-inflicted injuries, felony-related injuries, liability assumed by agreement, war, civil war, act of terrorism, radioactive and nuclear energy risks.

It should be noted that workers' compensation benefits do include cover for pain and suffering.

Usually, a time excess may apply, for instance the first 3 days of disablement.

Setting the benefit amounts or the liability limits

The amount of benefits payable to injured employees is usually set out and governed by Workmen's Compensation Acts or labour laws or labour protection regulations as the case may be. So compensation payments for injuries or deaths differ from one country to another.

Policy premium calculation

Workers compensation insurance premiums are calculated according to size of the employer's payroll, exposure to catastrophes both natural and man-made and how employees are classified. Classifications identify which type of work presents more risk, for example, rates for fast food restaurants would be lower than rates for fine dining restaurants. The Insured should check with the insurer what classification has been assigned to the business.

Some insurers may offer better rates if the Insured provides high quality employee training and management attitude is geared towards hazard detection and accident prevention.

A premium rate per one hundred dollar of salaries will be multiplied by the total estimated annual salaries of all employees to arrive at the annual policy premium.

What information do the insurers need to be told in an insurance application?

Insurers usual gather a small amount of information to price this policy relating to past accidents and claims experience, details of the business operation, number of employees, nature of employees work and their relationship to the employer's business.

SECTION 2

THE WORKMEN COMPENSATION INSURANCE POLICY

A COMMON MISCONCEPTION

Workers compensation insurance only covers injuries occurring on company premises!

Injuries that occur outside the workplace or even in an employee's home may be covered by the workers compensation policy if they arise out of employment and occur in the normal course of business. One such activity may be the sending and receiving of emails or working on a project or assignment at home.

Recent research findings and developing trends on work related injuries and compensation

In the UK, an estimated 17,000 workers withdrew permanently from the labor market annually as a result of work-related illness. In addition to their social costs, workplace injuries and illnesses also have a major impact on an employer's bottom line.

It has been estimated that US employers pay almost USD1 billion per week for direct workers compensation costs such as workers compensation payments, medical expenses and costs for legal services. The costs of workplace injuries and illnesses also include indirect costs such as accident investigation, training replacement employees and implementation of corrective measures, lost productivity, repairs of damaged equipment and property and costs associated with lower employee morale and absenteeism.

Research on the numbers and costs of occupational injury and illness in US found that fatal and non-fatal injury cases for low-wage workers in 2010 are estimated to be

596 and 1,625,152 respectively, with costs of USD441 million for fatal injuries and USD28 billion non-fatal injuries. In contrast, fatal and non-fatal illness cases are estimated at 12,000 and 88,000 respectively, with cost estimates of USD8.8 billion and USD1.5 billion respectively. For injuries and diseases combined, medical cost estimates are USD15 billion (39% of the total costs) and productivity costs are USD24 billion (61% of the total costs). Occupations contributing the greatest total costs, in order of chorological order, includes:

- retail salespersons
- janitors and cleaners
- maids and housekeeping cleaners
- stock clerks and order fillers
- combined food preparation and serving workers, including fast food
- cooks and restaurant
- cashiers

As evident from the above, workplace injuries are common in low wage occupations. Workers can receive burns, break bones, lose fingers or toes and even die in the course of employment.

Case Studies

The following claims scenarios highlight the range of potential accidents that could arise in the normal course of business.

CASE 1: A US court had ruled that a brewery worker was eligible for workers compensation benefits due to his addiction to alcohol. It seems that he had developed a daily habit of drinking 15 to 20 bottles of beer at work and more at home, not only that but his employer gave employees free beer to drink during their breaks at work.

SECTION 2

THE WORKMEN COMPENSATION INSURANCE POLICY

CASE 2: Courts in the USA have set precedence in that employees that are injured while playing sports on a company affiliated team are allowed to collect workers compensation benefits for injuries related to this activity.

CASE 3: Courts in the USA are endorsing that workers-on-demand or what is commonly referred to as independent-workers, for example, drivers used by car sharing businesses and drivers used in delivery of fast-food or parcels, are considered as employees of those businesses and must be insured under a workmen compensation policy to cover any on the job accidents.

THE INSURANCE
FIELD BOOK

Section 3

The Wider Picture

SECTION 3

40

Know Your Customer (KYC)

Many financial regulatory authorities around the world have a clear set of guidelines regarding the purchase of insurance products. The KYC has in many countries become a legal and mandatory requirement for individuals and businesses to fill-in before an insurance policy is sold.

Under such requirements, the insurer is required to demonstrate that it has identified the customer and verified its true identity and the nature of their customer's business by using reliable documents and information.

To achieve this requirement, insurers have to have in place processes enabling:

- The systematic collection and verification of identity information
- Customer name cross checking against certain lists (for instance, United Nations Terrorist List)

- Profiling a customer's expected transaction behavior
- Assessing the customer's perceived risk to commit money laundering and terrorism financing
- Continuous monitoring of a customer's transactions

Insurers are required to report to the authorities all suspicious transactions.

Why is a KYC required?

The main aims of the KYC are to prevent identity theft and the insurers being used in financial fraud, money laundering and terrorist financing.

Additionally, the KYC enables insurers to understand their customer needs better and to help them manage their risks prudently.

What documents should a business provide?

A business is minimally required to provide information on its location, legal entity, ownership, business activity and capital. Certain documents will be needed including:

- Commercial registration certificate, certificate of incorporation
- Partnership deed or Memorandum and Articles of Association
- Financial statements for last three years
- Licenses issued by the relevant authorities allowing transaction of business
- Utility bills and landline telephone bills
- Tax returns

Here are sample examples of when a red flag may be signaled by an insurer:

- Cancelling policy without a valid reason
- Overpayment of premium and subsequent requests for refund
- Fraudulent claims by the Insured with overestimated pricing
- Customer hesitation to supply information or providing fictitious details for identification
- Policies assigned to parties without any valid relationship with them
- Suspicious frequent changes in address

SECTION 3

KNOW YOUR
CUSTOMER (KYC)

41
Code of Ethics

The Merriam Webster Online Dictionary defines "Code of Ethics" as:

> *a set of rules about good and bad behavior.*

Individuals sometimes do not act in a way that is consistent with their moral beliefs, sometimes circumstances get in the way of moral perfection. The challenge for the industry has always been to gain the trust of those who purchase its products.

The insurance industry's traditional response to concern about consumer mistrust has been to stress objectives such as greater transparency and improved financial education. Insurance regulators, industry associations and institutions have additionally sought to fortify these objectives by introducing a code of ethics or conduct.

A set of rules is the framework of an expected good standard of business conduct in the sale of insurance products and in claims settlement aiming to provide fair treatment

SECTION 3
CODE OF ETHICS

to the Insured to win their trust and respect thereby enhance the industry's public impression and standing.

All insurance practitioners are required to abide by this code of ethics while those who violate its rules may become subject to disciplinary action.

Why does the insurance industry need a "Code of Ethics"?

The code is needed to protect customers against forced sales tactics, unfair treatment, misleading information, dishonest transactions, fraud and any conduct which may be considered improper for a professional.

A report published in 2014 has revealed that many consumers assume financial services businesses are 'all the same'. Interestingly, 39% of those surveyed, deemed personal experience dealing with the insurance provider as most influential factor effecting whether the provider was distrusted.

Who would such code apply to?

Well, basically all insurance related professionals at an individual level, from insurance company executives and directors to actuaries, consultants, brokers, sales agents, introducers and loss adjusters.

What behaviors does a code aims to prevent?

Insurance regulators, industry agencies and practitioners have sought to set high standards of conduct to prevent behaviors involving:

- Dishonesty by providing misleading or false information
- Unfair tactics in delaying or refusing claim

settlements
- Conflicts of interest
- Not applying due care and diligence in advising or serving the customer
- Exposing customer information that may be deemed confidential
- Lack of transparency
- Non-compliance with laws and regulations
- Slow and inefficient service
- Undue respect to customer complaints and protracting disputes

While no code can anticipate every possible situation, the central concept is surely to confirm the insurance practitioner's commitment to the principles of good and lawful conduct.

SECTION 3

CODE OF ETHICS

42

Insurance Intermediaries

These days there are many different ways to buy insurance and there are good reasons to consider using an insurance intermediary's expertise to help in making the best informed decisions.

Intermediaries are an essential element in the distribution and operations of insurance. They bring Insureds and insurers together, collect underwriting information for insurers, provide advice to Insureds, find and place insurance coverage and some could also assist with the claims process and risk management planning.

Intermediaries are especially valuable for commercial insurance buyers since many policies are customized and the price and terms are usually negotiated on a case-by-case basis. Larger intermediaries may be able to assist with risk modeling, risk management, management of captive insurance companies, asset management etc.

SECTION 3

INSURANCE INTERMEDIARIES

Regardless of the nature and size of the intermediary there are a set of requirements that business customers can expect to receive, for instance, intermediaries must help their clients understand and measure their risk, provide timely, complete and relevant information both before and after a contract is entered into. This includes the duty to sell the right types and amounts of insurance that are appropriate to their customers' needs.

Agents and brokers owe different levels of fiduciary duties to their clients. At the very least, they are expected to perform their work competently.

Who is an insurance intermediary?

An insurance intermediary is an individual or a firm that essentially assists in the purchase of insurance. The following are insurance intermediaries:

The Insurance agents

Those are individuals or firms that intermediate on the basis of an agency contract to sell insurance policies exclusively for one or several insurers. Insurance agents typically work for the insurance company in the insurance process, acting on behalf of the insurers not the customer.

In some markets agents are independent and work with more than one insurer and in others agents operate exclusively, either representing a single insurer in one geographic area or selling a different line of business for each of several insurers (but may not offer alternative policies of other insurers). Therefore they may be independent, tied or exclusive, insurer-employed or self-employed.

The Role of the Agent

The principal role of an insurance agent encompasses promoting, offering and underwriting the insurance policies of the insurer with which they have contractual ties.

An insurance agent will:

- Offer the products and services of a single insurer in the insurance line concerned in each case. An agent is not able to offer alternative policies of other insurers.
- Give advice to clients or prospective clients. The advice that an agent provides is limited to offering the best product, on the best terms for the client, among those offered by the insurer for which the agent works exclusively.
- Help the Insured maintain and review the policy covers in place.
- Give assistance in the event of a loss.

The Insurance brokers

Brokers are typically professional firms assisting buyers in choosing their insurance by offering options in both insurers as well as products. Acting as agent for the buyer, brokers deal with multiple insurers to obtain a particular coverage independent of insurers.

Broker's involvement in the insurance market is advantageous to both the buyer and the insurer, buyers get access to advantageous long term relationships built between brokers and insurers, advise on coverage offered by competing insurers, advise on the insurer's reputation for claims settlement, financial strength and risk management and insurers get important information gained by the broker on clients and clients' needs.

The Role of the Broker

Technically, a broker's role may change from "broker" to "agent of the insurer" during the insurance transaction and over the course of an ongoing relationship with the broker. For example, the broker acts on behalf of the buyer when negotiating the contract of insurance and placing the policy with the insurer but when the broker handles premium payments and claims settlements, the broker is essentially acting as agent for the insurer.

Engaging an insurance broker in the insurance selection process is vitally important to finding the best deal that the Insured requests or needs and further on to then providing day-to-day assistance on getting the very most out of the insurance policy.

A good insurance broker will:

- Comply with licensing and regulatory requirements and employ professionally qualified specialists.
- Have access to and strong relationships with the highly rated insurance carriers.
- Help the Insured identify and choose coverage that meets business needs.
- Report back and advise on the cost and coverage available from several insurers.
- Understand the Insured's business to ensure that all needs are adequately covered.
- Provide prompt technical advice when needed.
- Provide claims management facilities so that claims are negotiated quickly and diligently.
- Conduct regular review meetings ensuring business needs are regularly reassessed and that the market is reviewed well in advance of each policy renewal.
- Keep the Insured appraised of developments in the market, laws and regulations that may impact the insurance coverage in place.

Brokers invariably come in different sizes obviously offering different capabilities. Global broking firms handle insurance covers for multi-national businesses. Their activities include cover placement, risk assessment, loss mitigation, risk management and wholesale capabilities.

The smaller brokers tend to focus more on the retail functions and some tend to lack the sophisticated risk management capabilities of the much larger global brokers. Nonetheless, some are able to compete very strongly in handling local and regional business clients.

Tips on appointing and dealing with insurance intermediaries

When dealing with insurance intermediaries there are necessary qualities they should display and minimum service levels they should offer. Prior to entering into any relationship it is important to feel secure in the knowledge that the agent or broker is an honest and competent individual. Often, little thought is given to the act of appointing an insurance broker.

It is important that the person or firm being contracted has extensive experience in the area of insurance for which services are required. There are advantages in appointing an agent or a broker from a small firm. In most cases, personalized and prompt attention will be availed. In contrast, larger firms typically have greater resources in terms of service and manpower. The Insured should weigh the pros and cons of using a small or a large firm and whether to use a broker or an agent. It is crucial to make sure there is a team serving the Insured, who is in that team and that they are all capable and competent in serving the Insured.

The following should be taken into consideration:

- Ask for and check whether the intermediary holds a valid license and is authorized for the particular insurance product. Have proper credentials, including capacity, competence, proper training, honesty, and solvency. A professional designation like CIC, ACII or CPCU doesn't by itself guarantee an agent is expert in all the insurance aspects, but all other things being equal, a designation does signify the person has made a commitment to professional development.

- Check whether the intermediary has good knowledge of various insurance products.

- The intermediary accurately explains the scope of cover and exclusions.

- Beware of over-selling tactics. The Insured should not be asked to sign on a blank proposal form. Proposal forms should be filled up completely and comprehensively.

- Duly signed receipts are received immediately when premium payments are made through an Intermediary.

Paying for the services of intermediaries

The Insured must understand and be aware of costs and when payments are due when a policy is purchased and what deductibles are payable or when a claim is made.

Broker and agent compensation comprises premium based commissions, expressed as a percentage of the premium paid for each policy. Additionally, contingent commissions may also be involved, again usually expressed as a percentage of premiums, based on pre-agreed factors such as the profitability, persistency and volume of the business placed with the insurer. Premium-based commissions account typically for about 10-11% of premiums, compared with an average of 1-2% of premiums for contingent commissions.

Larger intermediaries may receive fees for particular services such as risk management, captive management, risk modeling and claims settlement services.

Intermediaries may get rewarded by insurers for superior performance in the form of non-cash compensation such as travel and vacation rewards.

What duties may the Insured have?

it is advisable that the Insured evaluates the intermediaries performance throughout the year and meet with them other than when the policy becomes due for renewal so that the Insured's needs are better highlighted rather than just the price of next year's policy.

Sharing expectations in terms of service and communication with the intermediary avoids dissatisfaction and missed opportunities. Equally important, is to make sure they understand Insured's growth plans and any new activities it might be undergoing.

After receipt of the policy, the Insured must check it thoroughly to ensure terms and conditions are identical to the offer requested and agreed to and if not, contact the intermediary and get them to explain or correct any differences. The Insured must be aware that the broker or agent may defend against a claim for breach of "duty of care" by relying on Insured's duty to read.

Insist on getting a written and detailed proposal of the insurance coverage before taking a decision. This may sound like an obvious point to a lot of business managers,

SECTION 3

INSURANCE INTERMEDIARIES

but it's a precaution some purchasers of commercial insurance fail to take notice of.

As the client of the agent or broker, the Insured certainly have a right to demand to know all the compensation that the agent or broker will receive from insurers if insurance business is placed through them. Full disclosure is something that a reputable agent or broker shouldn't object to and could be part of the decision making process.

The Insured is advised to insist on an annual written review of all existing policies and what additional coverage may be needed. If the intermediary is unwilling, or unable to provide this review, it may be a warning sign that the necessary level of insurance expertise and service are not being provided.

When can the Insured take legal action against a broker or agent?

If the Insured is convinced that it had been the victim of fraud or misrepresentation regarding the type of insurance it was sold, or what was covered and excluded, or if it was sold insurance that it did not need, or if the negligence or incompetence of a broker or agent has caused it financial loss because of a claim.

It should be remembered that both insurance brokers and agents owe a fiduciary duty of care to their clients. To succeed in an action against an insurance agent or broker, the Insured must prove that in addition to being negligent, the intermediary's negligence was a proximate cause of the loss.

For instance, liability for breach of fiduciary duty can occur if:

- broker neglects to obtain the proper insurance
- policy is void

- policy is materially deficient
- policy does not provide the coverage it undertook to supply

The success of a case against an insurance broker depends upon the unique facts of the case which must be carefully reviewed with an attorney.

SECTION 3

INSURANCE
INTERMEDIARIES

43

Professional Qualifications

The insurance industry is extremely competitive and agents and brokers face tremendous pressure to sell insurance products. High standards can sometimes be forfeited in order to ensure a sale goes through. There are also many cases when insurance agents and brokers had unwittingly given the wrong advice to customers.

Laws and regulations have sought to reinforce codes of ethics and practice but professional level education is surely expected to play a big role in ensuring that insurance practitioners are educated on industry ethics, technical aspects and selling skills. For an insurance practitioner, joining an industry specific institute will additionally improve their status within an area of expertise.

Many regulators around the world demand that if a person works in a regulated or a customer facing role, he/she must hold an insurance qualification or a product license to ensure that professionals who are advising customers are capable, ethical and confident in their work.

SECTION 3

PROFESSIONAL QUALIFICATIONS

All insurance professionals must be able to demonstrate that they have taken proactive steps to maintain their professional knowledge.

Employers, whether those are insurance companies, brokerages, independent adjusting firms or risk managers, are also increasingly encouraging advanced qualifications allowing employees to take advantage of opportunities for career progression into senior and more specialist roles. The knowledge and skills gained by most qualifications bring value to their organizations.

Certifications are usually earned from a professional society or educational institute, not through a governmental body. Various titles and designations are available depending on the status of the awarding institute and country. Chartered status is a sought after designation for insurance practitioners with some institutions offering a route to fellowship status. The Advanced Diploma or the ACII that is awarded by The Chartered Insurance Institute in the UK, is the world's most recognized insurance qualification while other designations such as the CPCU (Chartered Casualty and Property Underwriter) awarded by The American Institute For Chartered Property Casualty Underwriters is steadily gaining global popularity.

Recent developments have seen other qualifications developed and granted not only to individuals but also to institutions with some firms granted corporate chartered status by certain institutions.

Insurance designations should enable the customer to assess a broker's or an agent's expertise level. As the reader will see in the list below, different insurance designations have completely different focus. A well-established insurance broker could have different insurance specialists.

Best advice is to always seek the services of a well-qualified broker or agent who has been recommended through friends or colleagues.

Below is a partial list of the many professional qualifications available to insurance practitioners around the world:

Australia and New Zealand

THE AUSTRALIAN AND NEW ZEALAND INSTITUTE OF INSURANCE AND FINANCE - Certified Insurance Professional (CIP)

Canada

INSURANCE INSTITUTE OF CANADA - Chartered Insurance Professionals (CIP)

India

The Insurance Institute of India – Associateship Diploma (AIII)

Singapore

Singapore College of Insurance - Advanced Diploma in General Insurance and Risk Management (ADGIRM)

Switzerland

Insurance Institute of Switzerland - Chartered Insurance Broker (CIB)

United Kingdom

The Chartered Insurance Institute - The Advanced Diploma in Insurance (ACII)

Institute of Risk Managemen – Certified Member (CMIRM)

SECTION 3

PROFESSIONAL QUALIFICATIONS

The Chartered Institute of Loss Adjusters - Associate of the Chartered Institute of Loss Adjusters (ACILA)

Institute and Faculty of Actuaries - Associate of the Institute of Actuaries (AIA)

United States

The American Institute For Chartered Property Casualty Underwriters - Chartered Property Casualty Underwriter (CPCU)

The Society of Actuaries - Associate of the Society of Actuaries (ASA)

Life Office Management Association (LOMA) - Associate, Life Management Institute (ALMI)

Professional Liability Underwriting Society - Registered Professional Liability Underwriter (RPLU)

International Claim Association - Fellow, Life and Health Claims (FLHC)

International Foundation of Employee Benefit Plans - Certified Employee Benefits Specialist (CEBS)

44

Risk Management

Former President John F. Kennedy once said, "There are risks and costs to a program of action, but they are far less than the long-range risks and costs of comfortable inaction".

There are a lot of obvious and not so obvious risks for any business and business owners. Risk can come from both internal and external sources.

The external risks are those that are not in direct control of the management. These include political issues, exchange rates, interest rates, legal liabilities, credit risk, manmade accidents, natural disasters as well as deliberate attacks from an adversary and so on. Internal risks, on the other hand, include non-compliance or information breaches, server outage and lack of innovation among several others. The main types of risks are usually classified according to the following:

1. **Compliance risk**, for example the need to comply with food safety laws, accounting or tax rules.

2. **Financial risk**, refers specifically to the money flowing in and out of the business and the possibility of a sudden financial loss due for example from non-payment by a customer or increased interest charges on a business loan.

3. **Strategic risks**, this relates to business' strategy becoming less effective and as a result the business struggles to reach its goals. Examples of this maybe new competitors entering the market, shifts in customer demand, technological advancement, changes in the supply of raw materials, or any such large-scale changes.

4. **Operational risk**, for example customer dependency or the breakdown or theft of key equipment

5. **Reputational risk**, damage due to major product recall or an embarrassing law suit can cause an immediate loss of revenue

In a survey published in 2015, respondents were asked to rank the formidable risks facing their companies. This is how they were ranked:

- Damage to reputation or brand,
- Economic slowdown or slow recovery,
- Regulatory or legislative changes,
- Increasing competition,
- Failure to attract or retain top talent,
- Failure to innovate or meet customer needs,
- Business interruption,
- Third-party liability,
- Computer crime, hacking, viruses, malicious codes,
- Property damage.

All risk management processes involve several well defined steps:

Risk Identification

This is a thorough analysis of the business' operations and activities to identify what internal and external risks it is exposed to.

Evaluate risks and consequences

The business needs to decide which risks it will act upon and which risks it will ignore. A combination of qualitative and quantitative assessments investigate the likelihood of a risk or an event occurring against the potential impact or consequences.

Treatment of risks

This is also an exercise in balancing cost with consequences in identifying options available for treating or controlling the risk which may include action to avoid, reduce, share or retain the risk.

This involves considering risk control measures (for example insurance or fire detection alarms), deciding whether the existing measures are adequate, considering any additional measures that may be required and so on.

Monitor and review the process

It is important and an integral step in the risk management process to regularly review if there has been any change in the risk position, review the effectiveness of the treatment plan or strategies and, if necessary, repeat and review the whole process.

On top of high standard of risk assessment and identification programs, businesses do consider purchasing

SECTION 3

RISK MANAGEMENT

insurance as a way to mitigate damage that unforeseen threats can cause.

Buying insurance would be one of the parts of a risk management program. The Insured would be transferring some of the risks to an insurer. Well put together strategies for reducing risk can work together with insurance to reduce risk exposure.

For insurers, customers that have in place an effective and operational risk management practices demonstrates that a business is committed to loss reduction or prevention. Indeed, some risk management strategies may result in reduced insurance costs due to reduced likelihood of claims.

In recent years, many companies have added risk management departments to their organizations and a Chief Risk Officer (CRO) is tasked with carrying out the risk management process.

45

Reinsurance

The role of reinsurance isn't commonly known outside the insurance industry, interestingly however, insurance companies also buy insurance protection, called reinsurance. Reinsurance is a crucial loss sharing tool for insurers in which the insurer (usually referred to as the primary insurer or cedent) transfers (or cedes in reinsurance terms) part of its loss exposure to specialized professional reinsurers who have no primary business. The insurance buying public (the original policyholders) doesn't have to be aware of its existence as it takes place entirely between insurance and reinsurance companies.

The US, Germany and Switzerland are the most important domiciles for reinsurance companies but key players can also be found in Bermuda, France and at Lloyd's in London. Similarly, most reinsurance companies also purchase their own insurance and it is then called retrocession insurance.

Reinsurer's financial strength is one of the most important factors when primary insurers select the reinsurers they wish to deal with. The consequences of a financially

SECTION 3

REINSURANCE

unstable reinsurer could potentially mean claim reimbursement delays or even nonpayment. That's why insurance companies have come to rely more heavily on rating agencies to help them assess the financial standing of reinsurers. Rating agencies are third parties that specialize in looking at a variety of company metrics as well as regional, political, market and economic instabilities in the territory/s they reside and operate in and consequently assign a rate or a grade accordingly. Well known examples of such agencies include A.M. Best, Standard & Poors, Fitch, and Moody's.

So, why is reinsurance useful for insurance companies?

1. Insurers use reinsurance to offer larger limits of protection to an original policyholder. This allows the insurer to free up larger proportions of its capital.

2. Reinsurance offers predictability in short term and long term forecasting therefore smoothing out insurance company's results.

3. Reinsurers share a wealth of risk expertise with insurers in underwriting, risk management, claims and other areas. They can also forewarn insurers of particular emerging risks or developing claim patterns.

4. Reinsurers pay commission to the insurance company, the commission offsets the insurer's expenses.

5. Reinsurance arrangements reduce claims volatility guarding against extreme events and catastrophes thereby reducing the burden of severe claims.

There are two types of reinsurance agreements:

1. Reinsurance is arranged and agreed with a reinsurer or a group of reinsurers on individual risks or individual insurance policies. This case by case arrangement is commonly referred to as Facultative Reinsurance agreement or,

2. Reinsurance is automatically in place through an annual agreement with a reinsurer or a group of reinsurers reinsuring all new and renewal business of a certain class and under certain terms and conditions. The reinsurer must accept all business within the scope of this agreement which is commonly referred to as a Reinsurance Treaty.

Most insurance companies will use a combination of both types of agreements. Those two agreements also come in two different types, a proportional or a non-proportional type. The technical specifications of the two different types are beyond the scope of this book but for completion sake it's important to briefly outline the following differences.

In the proportional type of reinsurance agreements, the primary insurance company basically shares the same proportion of the premiums received and losses incurred with its reinsurers. This is a convenient arrangement and the primary insurer also receives a commission from the reinsurers against the premiums shared. The 'Quota Share' and the 'Surplus' agreements are examples of such proportional reinsurance.

In the non-proportional type of reinsurance agreements, the primary insurer is protected for an amount in excess of a specified retained portion of a loss or an accumulation of losses (for instance an event such as an earthquake causing damage to many policyholders at the same time).

SECTION 3

REINSURANCE

The retention of the primary insurer is a sort of deductible or an excess the insurer retains and the sum in excess of this retention is absorbed by the reinsurers up to a certain limit. The 'Per Risk Excess of Loss' and the 'Catastrophe Excess of Loss' agreements are examples of such non-proportional reinsurance.

THE INSURANCE
FIELD BOOK

Section 4

Four Ways Insurance is Getting Ahead in a Digital World

SECTION 4

Four Ways Insurance is Getting Ahead in a Digital World

It has been fascinating watching the meteoric changes the world of insurance has experienced in a few short years. Legacy insurers have had to look deep and hard into the potential effects of nimble new comers who continue to introduce fresh concepts in insurance and service.

A report released by Capgemini, "The World Insurance Report 2017" says technology is becoming integral to insurance with nearly one in three customers globally saying they use InsurTechs, either exclusively or in combination with incumbent firms.

SECTION 4

FOUR WAYS INSURANCE IS GETTING AHEAD IN A DIGITAL WORLD

InsurTech = Insurance + Technology

InsurTech is a term applied to the myriad of technologies used in disrupting the insurance industry by deploying smartphone apps, electronic personal wearables, telematics, pay-per-use insurance models, chat bots, artificial intelligence, blockchain, Internet-of-things and other innovations steering towards automating online policy handling and claims processing and changing the consumer expectations and demands delivering a fundamentally better experience.

Much of these new technological propositions are executed by startup companies aiming to squeeze out savings and efficiency from the current yet antiquated insurance industry model. These InsurTech companies are driven by the belief that the insurance industry is ripe for innovation and disruption.

The traditional insurance players lacked the incentive to exploit new technologies and as such the user experience is perceived as unsatisfactory. Nowadays, consumers expect insurers to provide broader coverage with personalized services that adapt to their behaviors and preferences.

Many of the startups though, have chosen to partner with global insurance companies. According to a PwC report*, about 90 percent of the insurers surveyed fear the loss of business to startups, with about 70 percent of insurance companies saying they have already taken action to face any new opportunity or challenge presented by InsurTech disruptors.

InsurTech startups are forcing the whole insurance industry to rethink how they do business and to become more innovative, more customer oriented and more transparent. This includes reinsurers, insurers, brokers, agents, third party administrators (TPA) and even loss adjusters. Two years ago, who would've thought changes would be so sweeping?

These changes can no longer be blamed on technological innovation, clients have changed too and so has expectations. In a way this new generation of clients has become a change catalyst to the industry.

Tomorrow's clients want to be able to get information, receive a quote and buy an insurance policy from the comfort of their office, home or even car via a smartphone in a matter of few minutes.

For incumbent insurers to meet these challenges its imperative that a comprehensive approach is used, including:

- Exploring and utilizing the latest tech innovations.
- Speeding up decision making to respond to trending changes. Ease of adaptation is a key attribute.
- Introducing better efficiencies and improving customer interactions through better customer profiling.

Recent innovative offerings can be categorized into the following:

1. BLOCKCHAIN

Blockchain technology is a decentralized distributed ledger of all transactions across a peer-to-peer network considered a secure storage and distribution solution. It provides financial services with transparency on records with a permanent time and date stamp, including titles, document histories, and notary services.

The protocol that is blockchain has enabled the transfer of value on the internet. You need to contrast file sharing with value transfer, for example, if you send a computer file to another person you are merely sending a copy of that file and you retain the original copy, but for the transfer of value such as cash, this would amount to double spending. Therefore, online transfer of cash had only been possible using middlemen or intermediaries such as PayPal and credit cards.

The blockchain protocol solved the double spend problem allowing for decentralized verification of transactions and ownership. The result is a decentralized ledger.

Smart contracts

These are essential ingredients of blockchain. A smart contract is a program that can store, verify, and execute the terms of a contract, for example an insurance policy. The smart contract contains a set of rules where one rule triggers subsequent actions until the contract is completed. These rules are stored in the blockchain and all related rules and actions should get reflected in the ledger. For both insurers and customers they offers the convenience of letting transactions be done between them directly, disintermediating the customer relationship.

Examples:

Dynamis, specializes in the area of smart contracts for insurance products relying on Ethereum, a decentralized platform that runs smart contracts. Dynamis sells supplementary unemployment insurance by using the LinkedIn social network as a reputation system. Applicants for a new policy can use LinkedIn to verify their identity and employment status. Likewise, claimants can use their LinkedIn connections to validate that they are looking for work.

Blockverify, works in the fraud detection area for goods such as diamonds, electronics, pharmaceuticals, and luxury items. Its solution allows users to check for counterfeit products, diverted or stolen goods, and fraudulent transactions. It works by labeling products creating their own register of products and then storing the history and supply chain in the blockchain. . Each product has a recorded history permanently recorded in the blockchain.

2. JUST-IN-TIME INSURANCE

Or on-demand insurance, gives customers the possibility and flexibility of buying insurance only when it is needed, reducing expenses and saving time. For example, a customer may be able to buy one hour's worth of auto insurance cover via a smart phone or tablet in few minutes for the exact period of time needed. While some form of usage-based insurance has been around for years, on-demand insurance still represents below 1% of the global insurance market.

This type of insurance is an innovation making insurance coverage literally a snap or a swipe through a mobile app. Surprisingly, these startups don't seem to be competing with incumbents. They are either reselling or enabling the value proposition of existing insurers.

While on-demand coverage is convenient and available at a better price, the per-item or per-use rates are largely higher than an annual (conventional) policy for those with wider needs or for those whose usage behaviors indicate higher risk profiles.

There's an element of behavioral economics involved here. The ability to turn insurance cover on and off is appealing to customers but are they going to make it a daily activity? And while certain times of day may be riskier than others, is there really a time when the customer doesn't want to be covered at all?

Examples:

Allstate, has secured a patent on what they called "Risk unit based policies". In practice, this allows the policyholder to buy a certain number of "risk units" that would be consumed while driving. If vehicle sensors detected someone was speeding, they'd use up more units than someone who wasn't. When the balance of units drops, the policyholder might get an alert through a mobile app, tablet or on a vehicle display. Policyholders would also receive tips on how they could reduce the rate of units that they consume, such as reducing speed, keeping a safer distance between vehicles and taking a less-busy route.

Trov, has developed an entirely mobile experience through a smart phone app making it possible to "protect just the things you want, exactly when you want, entirely from your phone," with no need for an insurance agent or a long-term contract. Users create an online inventory of what they consider valuable and then swipe on the items that they'd like to protect and choose a price and deductible that's right for them. Coverage is against accidental damage, loss and theft.

3. WEARABLE DEVICES

Wearable devices include miniature electronic devices that are worn or are somehow attached to the body to collect and transmit real-time data about the activity of the people wearing them. They include Bluetooth fitness trackers, smartwatches, wrist bands and even smart clothing and jewelry. The data collected helps insurers to continuously monitor customers' behavior and identify their needs and risks.

There are already some interactive devices in circulation, providing tangible support for conditions in need of constant management, such as mental health, return to work, obesity and diabetes. Effective apps and technology have the ability to reach broader population at low cost with highly effective results on health management and with surprising impact on mortality and morbidity. Wearable technology introduces a shift of dependency from healthcare professionals in hospitals and clinics to the individual in the community going about daily activities in managing health.

There are a number of companies seeking to create more accurate pricing models and build correlations between wearable data and health outcomes going beyond the traditional underwriting criteria to build in data sets from wearable devices.

Some InsurTech companies provide their devices to policyholders free of charge or at a discount and apply financial incentives for continued use of their devices.

The next generation of wearables will feature medical grade technology and will open the door to personalized health advice and targeted interventions.

Examples:

LifeSymb, uses artificially intelligent health robot, 3D depth cameras and accelerometers to collect movement data about a person in order to provide automatic health and fitness recommendations, without relying on a human expert. The recommendations are accessible on a smartphone or tablet allowing the users to connect with trainers and physiotherapists.

Vitality, a health and life insurer, helps its policyholders get active and earn rewards for doing so. Uses sensors in a smart watch to track wearer's sports activities. They have also partnered with 6,000 gyms and track policyholder's actual attendance from a swipe of their membership card.

4. PEER-TO-PEER (P2P) INSURANCE

This is when small groups of policyholders self-organize, pay premiums into a claims pool and self-administer their own insurance. If there's any money left in the pool at the end of the policy period, policyholders get a refund. Schemes are designed to increase transparency combined with incentives for policyholders to minimize claims thus helping to save customers time and money.

The idea of P2P is that a group of likeminded people with mutual interests, combine their insurance policies together encouraging a sense of control, trust, and transparency while at the same time saving costs. The core motivation is to mitigate conflicts that may exist in the traditional insurance relationship between insurers and policyholders as their incentives do no always align.

A new wave of P2P insurance adopting blockchain technology uses digital wallets where every member puts in their premium in an escrow type account only to be used if a claim is made. In this model, none of the members carry an exposure greater than the amount they put into their digital wallets. All payments in this model are done using bitcoin. Teambrella (described below) claims to be the first insurer using this model based on bitcoin.

The startups leading the development of P2P insurance are using group concepts to influence customer behavior, which means creating incentives for customers not to make false or exaggerated claims leading to the distribution of surplus at end of year.

Examples:

Friendsurance, this independent German insurance broker developed a concept to reward policyholders with cash-back bonus at the end of each year they remain claim free. Based on a shared economy approach, policyholders with the same insurance type form small groups. Part of their premiums is paid into a cashback pool. When claims arise, the cashback decreases for everyone. Small claims are settled with the money in the pool. Larger claims are settled by the standard insurance company covering any amount that exceeds the coverage through the group. They offer home contents, private liability and legal expenses insurance. Visit

Teambrella, Users of Teambrella provide coverage to each other by joining a team. Existing teammates decide how risky the new teammate is. If they deem the new teammate less risky, the payment will be than the average. Each teammate deposits funds into a special personal Bitcoin wallet. The funds in the wallet are co-controlled by the teammates. If the team votes to reimburse a teammate, all teammates pay their share from those wallets.

The digital transformation of the insurance industry is ongoing and it seems we're only looking at the beginning of the talent and money that will be invested into this major commercial sector. While InsurTech is playing catchup to the FinTech, there is no doubt that InsurTech could end up being as big if not bigger than Fintech and probably more disruptive.

FOUR WAYS
INSURANCE IS
GETTING AHEAD IN
A DIGITAL WORLD

Bibliography

Smith, Adam B., Matthews, Jessica L. Report never found. This information appeared in a report titled "Quantifying Uncertainty and Variable Sensitivity within the U.S. Billion-dollar Weather and Climate Disaster Cost Estimates". Marshall & Swift/Boeckh, 2011.

"Handling of insurance claims for Small and Medium sized Enterprises (SMEs) – May 2015, 2015". (PUB REF: 005056). Copyright permission received.

A thematic review TR15/6, *Financial Conduct Authority (FCA)*.

Fitch, G. A., Soccolich, S. A., Guo, F., McClafferty, J., Fang, Y., Olson, R. L., Perez, M. A., Hanowski, R. J., Hankey, J. M., & Dingus, T. A. "The impact of hand-held and hands-free cell phone use on driving performance and safety-critical event risk." (Report No. DOT HS 811 757). *Washington, DC: National Highway Traffic Safety Administration*, 2013, April.

www.distraction.gov/stats-research-laws/facts-and-statistics.html. Accesses 05.04.2016.

Distracted Driving, 2011.

"International Road Transport Union (IRU) funded by the European Commission". *A Scientific Study "ETAC" European Truck Accident Causation*, 2007.

Bressler, Martin, S. "The Impact of Crime on Business: A Model for Prevention, Detection & Remedy." *Journal of Management and Marketing Research*. Houston Baptist University, 2009, July.

Blevins, K, Kuhns, Joseph B. & Lee, S. *Understanding Decisions to Burglarize form the Offenders Perspective*, The University of North Carolina at Charlotte Department of Criminal Justice & Criminology, 2012.

Crime in the United States, 2007. United States Department of Justice, Federal Bureau of Investigation, 2008, September.

Top Business Risks. Top risks in focus: Business interruption, 2016. Allianz Risk Barometer 2016.

New Emerging Risk Insights. Swiss Re SONAR, May 2015.

Open for Business. Disaster Protection and Recovery Planning Toolkit for Small to Mid-sized Business. The Institute for Business and Home Safety, 2007.

When Trucks Stop, America Stops. American Trucking Association (ATA), 2015.

An Economic Analysis of Transportation Infrastructure Investment. National Economic Council and the President's Council of Economic Advisers, 2014.

www.rha.uk.net. Accessed 28.04.2016.

www.nationalarchives.gov.uk/doc/open-government-licence/version/3/. Accessed 28.04.2016.

"Loss trends and emerging risks for global businesses." *Global Claims Review 2014*, Allianz Global Corporate & Specialty, 2014.

2015 Data Breach Reports, report date: January 4th, 2016.

2015 Cost of Data Breach Study: Global Analysis Benchmark research sponsored by IBM, Independently conducted by Ponemon Institute LLC, May 2015.

Net Diligence Cyber Claims Study, 2014.

Coldstore Insulation-Panel Degradation. FJB Systems LLP. Accessed 10.04.2016.

Directors' liability D&O: Blurring the lines. A Survey conducted by Allen & Overy and Willis. September 2014.

Harris, C. IT "Downtime Costs USD26.5 Billion in Lost Revenue. Article appeared in Information Week, 2011". (CA Technologies). *InformationWeek.*

www.informationweek.com/it-downtime-costs-$265-billion-in-lost-revenue/d/d-id/1097919. Accessed 10.04.2016.

"Census of Fatal Occupational Injuries". *U.S. Bureau of Labor Statistics*, United States Department of Labor, 2012.

Costs to Britain of workplace fatalities and self-reported injuries and ill health 2013/14. Labour Force Survey (non-fatal injuries) and RIDDOR (fatal injuries), annual average estimate 2012/13- 2014/15. The Health and Safety Executive. Accessed 30.03.2016.

U.S. Senate Commerce Committee Report on Product Liability Reform Act of 1997. REPORT OF THE COMMITTEE ON COMMERCE, SCIENCE, AND TRANSPORTATION on S. 648 together with MINORITY VIEWS. U.S. GOVERNMENT PRINTING OFFICE WASHINGTON: 39–010. SENATE 105th Congress 1st Session REPORT 1997.

Zivin G., Neidell, J. & and Neidell, M. "The Impact of Pollution on Worker Productivity". *American Economic Review*, 102(7): 3652-73.2012, pp 22.

The World Health Organization (WHO), Geneva.

www.who.int/mediacentre/news/releases/2014/air-pollution/en/ and www.who.int/phe/health_topics/outdoorair/databases/FINAL_HAP_AAP_BoD_24March2014.pdf?ua=1 . Accessed 06.04.2016.

"Burden of disease from environmental noise. Quantification of healthy life years lost in Europe". *The World Health Organization, (WHO)*, European Centre for Environment and Health, Bonn Office and WHO Regional Office for Europe. JRC European Commission, 2011.

"Report to the Nations on Occupational Fraud and Abuse". *2016 Global Fraud Study.* The Association of Certified Fraud Examiners (ACFE), 2016.

"Who is the Typical Fraudster?" KPMG Analysis of Global Patterns of Fraud, 2011.

Occupational Fraud: A Study of the Impact of an Economic Recession. The Association of Certified Fraud Examiners, 2009.

"Loss trends and emerging risks for global business". *Global Claims Review 2014,* Allianz Global Corporate & Specialty, 2014.

Hall, J. *The Total Cost of Fire in the United States.* National Fire Protection Association, Quincy, MA. 2012, February.

Ahrens, M. *Lightning Fires and Lightning Strikes.* National Fire Protection Association, Fire Analysis and Research Division, 2013, June.

Campbell, R, *Structure Fires in Warehouse Properties.* National Fire Protection Association, Fire Analysis and Research Division, 2016, January.

"Insight into the next generation of employee benefits". *Sixth Annual Study of Employee Benefits: Today and Beyond*, Prudential Financial Inc., 2011.

"Employee Benefits in the United States". *National Compensation Survey (NCS)*, conducted by the U.S. Department of Labor, Bureau of Labor Statistics (BLS), March 2015. USDL-15-1432, July 24, 2015.

Bernheim, B., Carman K, Gokhale, J, Kotlikoff, L. *Are Life Insurance Holdings Related to Financial Vulnerabilities?* 2003.

Bernheim, B., Forni, L., Gokhale, J. & Kotlikoff L. "The Mismatch between Life Insurance Holdings and Financial Vulnerabilities". *Evidence from the Health and Retirement Study*, 2001.

2007-09 Panel Survey of Consumer Finances. Federal Reserve Board of Governors. Board of Governors of the Federal Reserve (2012).

Review of Maritime Transport 2011. United Nations Conference on Trade and Development (UNCTAD). United Nations Publication. UNCTAD/RMT/2011.

Bowden, A., & Basnet, S. *The Economic Cost of Somali Piracy 2011.* Working paper. One Earth Future Foundation. Oceans Beyond Piracy (OBP), 2011.

World Bank 2013. *Pirate Trails: Tracking the Illicit Financial Flows from Pirate Activities off the Horn of Africa.* A World Bank Study. Washington, DC: World Bank. DOI: 10.1596/978-0-8213-9963-7.

SE Asia tanker hijacks rose in 2014 despite global drop in sea piracy, IMB report reveals (12.01.2015). The International Chamber of Commerce (ICC) International Maritime Bureau (IMB), 2014.

Graham, P. *Casualty and World Fleet Statistics as at 01.01.2016. Total Loss Trends.* IUMI Facts & Figures Committee. International Union of Marine Insurance

(IUMI). (Source: LLI, total losses as reported by Lloyds List), 2016.

Copsey, S. *A Review of Accidents and Injuries to Road Transport Drivers.* European Agency for Safety and Health at Work (EU-OSHA). Luxembourg: Publications Office of the European Union, 2010.

Carstensen, G., Hansen, W., Hollnagel, V., Hojgaard, H., Jebsen, Ib, Knies, P., Klit, L., Kofoed, P., Mikkelsen, B., Petersen, K., *Lastbiluheld – en dybdeanalyse af 21 uheld*, Analysegruppen for Vejtrafikuheld (AVU) rapport No. 3, 2001.

A Scientific Study "ETAC" European Truck Accident Causation. International Road Transport Union (IRU), European Commission, 2007.

Kuratorium für Verkehrssicherheit, Ladung richtig sichern, Verkehr und Mobilität, 2005.

Kuratorium für Verkehrssicherheit, Rollendes Risiko, Verkehr und Mobilität, Unfallursachen: Mangelnde Ladungssicherheit, 2008.

American Entrepreneurship: Dead or Alive? An article by Jim Clifton appeared on Gallop website. www.gallup.com/businessjournal/180431/american-entrepreneurship-dead-alive.aspx. Accessed 02.03.2016.

Bradley III, D. & Cowdery, C. *Small Business: Causes of Bankruptcy.* University of Central Arkansas & University of Central Arkansas. citeseerx.ist.psu.edu/viewdoc/download?doi=10.1.1.367.4484&rep=rep1&type=pdf. Accessed 01.03.2016.

Becker, S. and Hvide, H. "Do Entrepreneurs Matter?" *Working Paper.* IZA DP No. 7146. January, 2013.

"Loss trends and emerging risks for global business". *Global Claims Review 2014,* Allianz Global Corporate & Specialty, 2014.

Trivella, A. Mitigating *Equipment Breakdown Risks*, May 30, 2008.

Arnold, A. "Assessing the Financial Impact of Downtime". *Business Computing World.* 20.04.2010. www.business-computingworld.co.uk/assessing-the-financial-impact-of-downtime/. Accessed 10.04.2016.

Ortashi, O., Virdee, J., Hassan, R., Mutrynowski, T. & Abu-Zidan, F. "The practice of defensive medicine among hospital doctors in the United Kingdom". *BioMed Central Ltd.* 2013.

Wallace, E., Lowry, J., Smith, S. & Fahey, T. "The epidemiology of malpractice claims in primary care: a systematic review." *BMJ Open*, 2013.

Starfield, B, *Is US health really the best in the world?* Department of Health Policy and Management, Johns Hopkins School of Hygiene and Public Health. July 26, 2000.

Blevins, K., Kuhns, J. & Lee, S. *Understanding Decisions to Burglarize form the Offenders Perspective.* The University of North Carolina at Charlotte Department of Criminal Justice & Criminology, 2012.

Liberty Mutual Workplace Safety Index. Liberty Mutual Research Institute for Safety, 2016.

Mullins, L. *The Top 5 Causes of Accidental Home Injury Deaths and How to Prevent Them.* Aug. 31, 2009.

"A Resilient City: Building cities able to withstand and recover from crises." *UN Habitat.* mirror.unhabitat.org/categories.asp?catid=690. Accessed 25.04.2016.

"10 costliest earthquakes ordered by insured losses". *Loss events worldwide 1980 – 2014*. Munich Re. As at January, 2015.

Direct Line analysis of YouGov and Office for national Statistics data covering SME numbers and professional indemnity cover for 2013 and 2014, conducted in August 2015.

Research conducted online by *Consumer Intelligence for Direct Line for Business*. www.directlineforbusiness.co.uk/news/risky-businesses-two-thirds-of-smes-unprotected Accessed 24.04.2016.

US District Courts.

Consumer Product Safety Commission (CPSC). www.cpsc.gov/en/Business--Manufacturing/Civil-and-Criminal-Penalties/. Accessed 28.04.2016.

"Measuring and Understanding the Impact of Terrorism". *The Global Terrorism Index*. The Institute for Economics and Peace (IEP), 2015.

2015 Terrorism Risk Insurance Report. Marsh LLC. Insights, June 2015.

The European Payment Report. Intrum Justitia AB, 2015.

International Trade Survey. Report is supported by The Institute of Export, undertaken by Trade & Export Finance Ltd. and sponsored by AIG, May 2014.

"Costs to Britain of workplace fatalities and self-reported injuries and ill health, 2013/14." *Labour Force Survey, annual average 2008/09 to 2011/12, 2014/15*. The Health and Safety Executive First published 10, 2015.

Leigh, J. *Numbers and Costs of Occupational Injury and Illness in Low-Wage Occupations*. White paper. Center for Poverty Research, and Center for Health Care Policy and Research, University of California Davis, USA, December, 2012.

Borkowski, L., & Monforton, C. *Mom's Off Work 'Cause She Got Hurt: The Economic Impact of Workplace Injuries and Illnesses in the U.S.'s Growing Low-Wage Workforce*, 2012.

Stand out for the right reasons. How financial services lost its mojo – and how it can get it back. PricewaterhouseCoopers LLP. 2014.

Cummins, D. & Doherty, N. *The Economics of Insurance Intermediaries*. Wharton School. University of Pennsylvania. May 20, 2005.

Regino, v. Aetna Cas. & Sur. Co., 200 N.J.Super. 94, 99, 490 A.2d 362 (App.Div.1985) superseded by statute on other grounds as stated in Strube v. Travelers Indem. Co. of Ill. (T.I.L.), 649 A.2d 624 (N.J.Super.Ct.App.Div.1994).

Global Risk Management Report. AON, 2015.

"Opportunities await: How InsurTech is reshaping insurance". *Global Fintech survey*. PwC, June 2016.